GROWING UP
PSYCHIC

GROWING UP
PSYCHIC

My Story of Not Just Surviving but Thriving
—and How Others Like Me Can, Too

CHIP COFFEY

THREE RIVERS PRESS
NEW YORK

Published in the United States by Three Rivers Press, an imprint
of the Crown Publishing Group, a division of Random House,
Inc., New York.

www.crownpublishing.com

Three Rivers Press and the Tugboat design are registered
trademarks of Random House, Inc.

Library of Congress Cataloging-in-Publication Data

Coffey, Chip.
    Growing up psychic : my story of not just surviving but thriving—
and how others like me can, too / Chip Coffey.
        pages cm
  1. Children—Psychic ability. 2. Parent and child. 3. Coffey, Chip.
I. Title.
    BF1045.C45C65 2012
    133.8092—dc23
    [B]

                                                            2011049425

ISBN 978-0-307-95674-3
eISBN 978-0-307-95675-0

Printed in the United States of America

Design by Maria Elias

10 9 8 7 6 5 4 3 2

This book is dedicated to every person who has suffered the pain of intolerance, indifference, bigotry, prejudice, hatred, and/or abuse.

I pray to God that, someday, our world will be a different, kinder, better place.

Amen.

^i^

They live among us. They are very real and they look just like you and me. They number in the thousands, perhaps millions. In the past, they used to hide in the shadows and carefully guard their secrets, but now, more and more children with paranormal abilities are "coming out of the psychic closet" in vast numbers and refusing to remain silent.

What can we do to help these psychic kids? Sadly, no one really knows the answer to that question, but until mainstream society at least acknowledges their existence, we cannot even begin the process. And very little will change. They will continue to be misunderstood, mistreated, misdiagnosed, and considered misfits.

The time has come to recognize that these children do exist. They need our understanding and our guidance because right now, at this very moment, there are children and families in crisis.

That's why I wanted to write this book: to rattle some cages and continue the process of educating the public about psychic kids. It is my hope that I can help to change the ways psychic children—and all true psychics—are perceived and treated.

CONTENTS

CONTENTS

CONTENTS

FOREWORD

In this delightfully engaging book, my friend Chip Coffey discusses a puzzling, enormously portentous, and yet quite common kind of occurrence: seemingly normal kids who say that they see spirits or talk to dead people. I hear from parents with stories like these all the time, and generally they are curious about what's happening to their child, but even more, they are worried. They worry that their child might be mentally ill or disturbed despite the fact that otherwise the child seems perfectly okay.

Chip Coffey's book will be very useful for these parents, I believe, and a source of comfort and reassurance. He offers insightful observations and practical tips about how to handle this perhaps strange-seeming, but nonetheless remarkably frequent, set of circumstances.

I could relate plenty of cases like those Chip describes in this book, but instead, I would like to share what happened to me with two of my own kids. My wife, Cheryl, and I don't talk about life after death. Talking about life after death is my profession, something I do when I am on the road on lecture tours. At home, Cheryl and I talk about what we are having for dinner that night. We talk about how we are going to pay the phone bill. We talk about what to do about our kids' homework assignments. In sum, we just talk about normal, regular, everyday family things. Plus we don't go to church, so our children have grown up insulated from speculations about the afterlife.

Nevertheless, things have happened with our two young kids, both adopted at birth, that thrilled, inspired, and astonished me beyond words. When my son, Carter, was five years old, he and I were sitting together on the bed watching television. I was flipping through the channels with the remote control. As I flipped past what turned out to be the National Geographic Channel, Carter suddenly became very animated. "Dad! Dad! That's my village!" he shouted.

When I turned back to the channel, a documentary about village life in China was playing. Carter started chattering away about the life he had lived in China with his previous mother, father, and siblings. Then, obviously realizing that I was utterly dumbstruck and baffled, he paused to orient me.

"Yeah," he said, "and then I was up in the air and I looked down and I saw you and Mom lying in the grass." To make a long story short, five years before Carter was born, Cheryl and I were touring Greece. One day when we were visiting an archaeological site and were really tired, the guard at the site invited us to lie down on the grass and take a nap. As we were lying there, we began talking about our desire to adopt a child.

The same kind of thing also happened with my daughter, Carol Ann, when she was nine years old. Together these incidents absolutely convinced me that our children came specifically to us, albeit not by the biological route, but by a spiritual pathway instead.

I know that many, many other parents have had these same kinds of life-changing spiritual experiences with their own children, and my hope is that in the future academia won't be as timid or rigid as it is today and serious, rigorous scholarly investigation will be supported for these experiences and the biggest question of human existence, life after death.

Exciting, authentically rational new means of studying the question of life after death are on the horizon, but for now, read Chip Coffey's book to learn about an astonishing, inspiring, unexplained propensity of the human mind.

—Dr. Raymond Moody, author of *Life After Life*

GROWING UP
PSYCHIC

Growing Up Psychic— My Own Story

I have often heard the old adage that one should write about what one knows. If that's true, this is the book I was born to write. Growing up psychic is a subject I know very well, because it is precisely what I did: I grew up psychic.

It is my belief that everyone is, in some manner, psychic or intuitive or sensitive. You choose the word. Psychic ability is the sixth sense with which I believe every one of us is born.

My own psychic abilities manifested when I was very young. My family tells me that when I was a very small child—before I can actually remember—I would frequently stare at the telephone, mention a name, and that person would call shortly thereafter. When telling people about this early ability, I've often joked that I was the original caller ID.

Perhaps my "psychic destiny" was written long before I was born. My maternal great-grandmother was a Native American medicine woman whose own abilities were widely known throughout the Southeast during the early years of the twentieth century. And my mother also had unique abilities that she believed she'd inherited from her grandmother.

Some people believe that we plan our life prior to incarnating into the "living world." If that is true, I certainly chose a difficult beginning. My mother always maintained that she'd had a near-death experience during my birth. She'd had a previous child who died when he was less than one day old as a result of complications during his difficult delivery. When it came time for my own birth, I was trapped inside her womb by the scar tissue that had formed there, and the doctors had to perform a Cesarean section to get me out. While my mother was on the operating table her blood pressure suddenly plummeted. She later told me that she'd heard a nurse say, "We're losing her," and, at that moment, two beautiful angels in white robes appeared, took her by the arms, and started to lift her off the table. She begged the angels not to take her because she wanted to stay with me, and as they returned her soul to her body, I was born.

So, based on my ancestry and the way I came into this world, you could say that being psychic is in my DNA.

Both my parents had deep Southern roots, but I was born in Elmira, New York, where they had moved after visiting my dad's sister, my aunt Polly, and her husband, Kenneth, who was from Elmira. I was baptized into the Catholic faith at Saints Peter and Paul Catholic Church in Elmira, but we moved back "home" to Spartanburg, South Carolina, shortly after my first birthday. There, my parents opened a traditional 1950s-style café called the Be-Bop, complete with a pinball machine and a Wurlitzer jukebox loaded with records by contemporary music icons like Elvis Presley, Connie Francis, the Everly Brothers, Fats Domino, and the Platters. I was a precocious child; I learned to read and to write—both printing and cursive—by the time I was three or four years old. I excelled in school and I loved to read. When I was seven, my parents sold the Be-Bop and we moved into a lovely home in the suburbs of Spartanburg. Tragically, however, it was destroyed by fire a couple of years later, and soon after that my parents decided to move back to Elmira.

That's when they bought the Murphy house, which had been built in the mid-1800s by Michael and Mary Murphy to house them and their five children—James, Mary Frances, Bridget, Margaret, and William. Margaret, the last of the Murphy clan, died in 1964, and my parents bought the house from her estate. Needless to say, after a century of continued occupation, the place had fallen into disrepair. So our entire family, including my aunt and uncle and their son, my cousin Kenny, went to work renovating it from top to bottom. When we got done, it was a real showplace, but after a couple of years my father once again wanted to move back to South Carolina. A country boy at heart, he had always longed to live again on a farm.

A few days after he put the Murphy house up for sale, my father received a call from the Realtor who had been doing the necessary title search. It seemed that there was a potential Murphy heir unaccounted for. A brief entry in the abstract of the title mentioned a sixth child, John, who was apparently the eldest son of Michael and Mary. According to the abstract, John had disappeared sometime in the mid-1880s, never to be heard from again. So, until it was proved that he had no living heirs who could claim the property, my parents didn't legally own the house, despite the fact that they'd paid for it and received a deed. The Realtor told them that they would have to place advertisements in newspapers across the country and wait for a period of six months. If, after that time, no heir came forward, they would receive a deed free and clear.

While we were waiting, my mother decided to do some investigating on her own. She and I spent hours combing through old newspapers in the basement of the local library, and what we discovered was absolutely fascinating. James, Michael and Mary's oldest known son, had been murdered in 1898. According to the newspaper, James and another young man had argued just a few blocks from the Murphy house, and James was stabbed to death. His murder had created quite a stir in Elmira, with daily accounts of the investigation, the suspect's arrest, and the subsequent trial featured in the newspaper. We also discovered information about another tragic death. Daughter Bridget had fallen down the stairs in the Murphys' house, broken her neck, and died at the age of five. What we didn't find, however, was any mention of the elusive John.

Mother and I even visited the local Catholic cemetery, hoping to find him buried there along with the rest of his family. We found the graves of all the others in the Murphy family, but not John's. His whereabouts still remained a mystery. In fact, we were beginning to wonder if John had ever existed.

During this time, strange things started happening in the house. Whether or not our sleuthing in the library had awakened long-dormant spirits, I can't say for sure, but the lights in the huge brass chandeliers that hung in both the dining room and the formal living room started to turn themselves on and off. We heard music being played on the spinet piano in the empty living room. There was suddenly a "cold spot" in the archway between the living room and the den that never warmed up even though there was a heat vent only steps away. At Christmastime, pinecone decorations we'd placed on top of the television began to levitate several inches into the air and then lower themselves back onto the TV.

Dad called in a team of ghost hunters from nearby Cornell University who verified the cold spot and placed a tape recorder on a table in the hallway. With the tape recorder left running, we all went out to dinner, and when we returned the voice of a little girl could be heard on the tape along with the voice of a man whom she identified as her father. We also heard piano music in the background and the sound of a steam locomotive, even though no trains had run on the nearby tracks for more than a decade. The ghost hunters determined that the house was "definitely haunted"—a conclusion that even I, at the age of thirteen, considered the understatement of the century.

My parents ultimately received their free-and-clear deed in the spring of 1968, and the house sold quickly. By the end of August, we were packed up and ready to move. As we were taking a last look around while our belongings were being loaded into the moving van, my mother mentioned that she'd miss the house and all its ghosts, so my father suggested that we invite them along. As we were walking out the door he called back, "You're welcome to come with us if you want to, as long as you behave yourselves." It didn't take long for us to discover that they had accepted his last-minute invitation.

Shortly after we moved into our new home, while my parents and a bunch of our relatives were busy unpacking, someone volunteered to take us kids to the movies to get us out from underfoot. I'd brought a clean shirt into the living room to change into so that I'd be "presentable" for our trip to town and had just laid it on a table when it spontaneously rose up and floated halfway across the room before dropping onto the floor. We all looked at one another as my father smiled and said, "Well, I guess the Murphys took me up on my offer." That's actually the last concrete sign we had from the Murphys, but I've always continued to feel a special kinship with them.

FINDING MARGARET MURPHY

One of the few items left in the Murphy house when my parents bought it in 1965 was an Irish greeting mounted in a plain dark wood frame that we found hanging by the front door. The greeting reads:

> The house is yours,
> Its portal opens wide
> And welcomes you to all inside.
> Dear friend and guest,
> Enter in peace and rest,
> The house is yours.

It has been several decades since I moved from the Murphy house and ever since, this framed greeting has hung near the front door of every place that I have called home.

In the mid-1990s, I decided to take apart the frame in order to polish the wood and clean the glass. (Don't ask why I hadn't done this before. I hate housecleaning!) I removed the tiny nails that secured the cardboard backing to the frame and made an amazing discovery.

Hidden behind the Irish greeting was a photograph of a lovely dark-haired young woman wearing a high-necked lace blouse with a buttoned-up silk overgarment. I assumed that she had to be one of the Murphy women, which was confirmed when I showed the photo to several people who had been neighbors of the Murphys back in Elmira.

The woman in the photo is Margaret, the youngest daughter and last of the Murphy clan, since, strangely enough, none of the children ever married. I've often wondered why her photo was hidden so many years.

I had the greeting reframed and placed the photograph of Margaret back in the original frame. Both are now hanging, side by side, in the foyer of my home in Georgia, a constant reminder of the family I never met in life but about whom I'd learned so much after their deaths.

After leaving Elmira, my family moved to a thirty-two-acre farm in rural South Carolina. In addition to the sprawling wooden farmhouse that had been built at the turn of the twentieth century, there was a small boathouse on the shore of a lake, a barn for the horse and Shetland pony my father had bought me, and, in the woods near the house, the ruins of an old log fort that we'd been told was built in the late 1700s. It was a rather idyllic, although sometimes lonely, life for a teenage boy.

One spring day not long after we'd moved in, we had a couple of unexpected visitors. A car came down the winding dirt road that led to the house, and an elderly man and a middle-aged woman got out. The man introduced himself by saying that he lived on the farm as a young boy and had asked his daughter to take him back to see it. We invited them to come inside to take a look around, and it was fascinating to watch the expressions on the old man's face as he revisited the past, with memories of days long ago replaying in his mind. Later, while sitting at the kitchen table and sipping a glass of lemonade, he told us that he'd actually lived in the fort until his father and uncle built the farmhouse. Then he asked a puzzling question: "Did you ever see anything strange in the woods?"

When my father asked what he meant by that, the old man took a deep breath and launched into his story. It seemed that he and his sister had been playing in the woods not far from the fort one day at just about sundown when they heard a rustling in the trees and turned to see what he called "this thing" standing upright and covered with long shaggy hair staring at them. The terrified kids ran home to tell their father, who went back out to see if he could find anything. But all he saw were "some weird tracks in the dirt" that looked sort of like three-toed hoofprints.

My father admitted that he and my mother had also seen some unusual footprints in the mud down by the lake. He said that they were pretty small but that when he'd stepped in the mud next to one, his foot didn't sink down nearly as deep, which he took to mean that whatever had made the prints was much heavier than he was.

"Then he's still here," the old guy said, shaking his head. "We used to call him the Wangdoodle, but my grandma insisted it was the devil."

At that point I was ready to pack up and leave the farm forever, but my parents assured me, after the man and his daughter had gone, that the creature was nothing but a figment of the old man's fanciful imagination and the prints my father had found were no doubt made by some kind of wild animal. Then, several weeks later, I was home alone one evening when the dogs outside suddenly started to growl and bark their heads off. Someone—or some*thing*—was walking on the front porch. I ran through the house locking all the doors and, on my way back to the living room, grabbed my dad's handgun from the drawer of his bedside table. I collapsed back onto the couch and held my breath as I heard the screen door creak and the knob on the front door slowly begin to turn. I yelled that I had a gun, and after a moment I heard the screen door closing and lumbering footsteps leaving the porch. I sat frozen in place until my parents got home. When I frantically described what had happened, my parents took me out on the porch to investigate. We were all shocked by what we found. There, on the painted wooden boards, was a trail of muddy footprints just like the ones my mom and dad had seen near the lake. So what was this "thing"? A wild animal, as my father had insisted? A Bigfoot, yeti, or Sasquatch? The Wangdoodle? Or was the old man's grandma correct after all? I still don't know the answer, but, thankfully, the creature never returned.

My interest in things paranormal, which had begun with the phenomena we'd experienced in Elmira, grew over the next several years. *Dark Shadows*, which was at the time a wildly popular television soap opera whose supernatural characters included vampires, werewolves, and warlocks, captured not only my imagination but also the imagination of practically every kid I knew. We were all avid viewers, and I became fascinated by the idea of time travel, making predictions based on the use of tarot cards, and all things occult. I desperately wanted to own a deck of tarot cards, which wasn't easy to come by in Spartanburg in the 1970s and well before the advent of Internet shopping, but I finally found one in a small shop filled with an eclectic collection of odds and ends and taught myself to read them. I had a subscription to *Fate*, a magazine devoted to the occult, and I was reading about Nostradamus and Edgar Cayce as well as Ruth Montgomery's biography of famed psychic Jeane Dixon. A friend of my mother's did card readings and handwriting analysis, and I was very curious to know more about these things. I'd sometimes use tarot cards or psychometry (feeling the energy of an object) to do readings for my parents' friends and my family, and, from time to time, I'd spontaneously tell my friends about something that was going to happen before it actually occurred. One particular memory I have is of being ten years old when one of my mother's friends said she had something to tell me and I spontaneously asked, "When is the baby due?" without knowing that she was pregnant.

Then, when I got to Elmira College, I found that many of my contemporaries were interested in these things as well. We were studying Jungian psychology and the religions of various cultures, and we were fascinated by the concept of reincarnation and past-life experiences.

I still had no idea that I had the ability to communicate with those in spirit, although I did realize that I sometimes had the ability to know things before they occurred, an ability known as precognition. I knew this was part of who I was, but I didn't particularly consider it weird or unusual. Because many of my friends were also interested in mysticism and the supernatural, I continued to do some tarot readings and psychometry with them, but it certainly never occurred to me then to turn my gift into a career choice.

I've worked in many industries over the years. As a child, I worked as an actor and a model. I've been a traditional counselor, and I've worked as a social worker and handicap services coordinator for Head Start, a federally funded preschool program for low-income families. I've had successful careers in both the entertainment and hospitality industries, and I was working in travel management while also doing some psychic readings by phone on the side to make extra money when the events of 9/11 occurred, sending the travel business into a state of free fall. As a result, I lost my job as a travel agent, and as I was walking out of the building for the last time, carrying my personal belongings in a cardboard box, I said to myself, "Well, Chip, it looks like you're a full-time psychic medium now."

Truthfully, I had absolutely no idea whether I'd be able to support my lifelong habits of living indoors and eating on a regular basis by doing psychic readings. But at the same time, I knew somewhere deep within me that the universe had just provided me with the opportunity to do what I'd been afraid to do on my own—and, as I now realize, what I was destined to do my entire life!

I started doing some local events, like small psychic fairs, which quickly evolved into regional and national conferences and conventions. My career as a professional psychic and medium was starting to take off, and when I met the renowned ghost hunter Patti Starr, I added "paranormal investigator" to my résumé.

I met Patti through a paranormal-related website in 2002 and was intrigued when I read in her profile that she had grown up in a small town in South Carolina not far from where I had lived as a child. We began exchanging e-mails and soon progressed to chatting by phone. I learned that Patti was the founder of an investigative group called Ghost Chasers International, located in Lexington, Kentucky, and was very excited when she invited me to join them for an investigation at a place called the Bishop's House in Lexington. "You're welcome to stay with my husband, Chuck, and me, but I have to warn you that our guest room is haunted," she told me. Despite the fact that I really don't like sleeping all by myself in haunted locations, I graciously—and somewhat hesitantly—accepted Patti's invitation.

I drove to Kentucky and met the members of Patti's group when they assembled at her house prior to the investigation. While we were all talking, something very strange occurred. The cell phone of Jason Lewis, one of Patti's group members who is also a psychic and medium, began to ring. He looked to see who was calling and his jaw dropped in amazement. "You are not going to believe this," he said, walking toward me. I looked down at Jason's phone, and caller ID revealed that the incoming call had been placed from my cell phone, which was impossible because my phone was on the counter in Patti's kitchen. Even stranger was the fact that I had met Jason less than an hour earlier and did not even know his cell phone number. There was absolutely no rational explanation for how this could have happened.

Before we all left for the investigation, Patti briefed us on the history of the Bishop's House. It had been the home of the local Episcopal bishop from the late 1800s to the mid-1960s. The house was later sold by the church and converted into an apartment building. The current owner, a young man named Stuart, had contacted Patti to request an investigation of the house. Prior to purchasing the property, he had not known about its reported history of hauntings, but he soon discovered that others in the community did know.

Employees of the gas, electric, and water companies refused to go into the basement in order to read the meters. Some contractors and home repairmen were also hesitant to enter the building. Once, when

Stuart's father was helping him with repairs in the basement, he asked his son, who he thought was standing behind him, to hand him a wrench. Without looking back, he held out his hand and the wrench was placed in it. Moments later, he turned to speak to Stuart and was surprised to find that he was not there. He called out to his son and was flabbergasted when Stuart answered from the floor above.

Several other strange incidents had occurred at the Bishop's House. The tenant of one apartment reported returning home one evening to find all the candles in her apartment had been lit when no one had been there. Another tenant claimed that the cabinet doors and drawers in his kitchen would constantly open on their own. It certainly appeared as if the place was, indeed, haunted, and we hoped to confirm that or find some other explanation.

Our investigation lasted for several hours, and later I would describe the experience as my baptism by fire into the strange world of ghost hunting. I was intrigued by all the equipment Patti and her team members used, including meters that detected electromagnetic fields and laser thermometers that tracked sudden changes in temperature, as well as digital and video cameras and audio recorders.

At one point during the investigation, several of us were standing in the dark foyer of the Bishop's House. The only light came from the viewfinders of the video cameras a couple of people were holding. Unexpectedly, someone took a photo with a digital camera and in the light from the flash, I saw a little girl with long blond hair wearing an old-fashioned dress standing beside me! Startled, I shouted out, "Holy $#&@! Did anyone else see that little girl standing next to me?" I was relieved when others said that they, too, had seen her.

When Patti, her husband, and I returned to their home in the wee hours of the morning, I went downstairs to the guest room, but the strange things I'd experienced at the Bishop's House, coupled with the fact that Patti had informed me her basement was also haunted, made it virtually impossible for me to sleep.

A few weeks later, Patti called to inform me that Stuart had told her about another strange incident that had occurred since our visit. His telephone rang one day and when he answered, a little girl's voice asked, "Can Chloe come down and play with me?"

"You must have the wrong number. There's no little girl named Chloe here," he told her gently. Then, a few minutes later, Stuart's phone rang again.

"I want Chloe to come down and play with me," the same small voice said.

"Honey, I told you before, there's no one here named—" Stuart began, then stopped when he realized that perhaps the child was talking about his dog, whose name was Chloe. In fact, he'd noticed that Chloe had recently begun to act strangely whenever she went into the foyer, as if she were looking at something or someone he couldn't see, then wagging her tail and running around like she was playing. "Are you talking about my dog, Chloe?" he asked. And then the phone line disconnected.

"Stuart thinks that maybe his dog sees the little girl you saw in the foyer of his house," Patti told me. "And as crazy as it sounds, it appears that she called Stuart to ask if Chloe could come down to the foyer to play with her."

Cue the theme from *The Twilight Zone*!

A couple of years later, Patti and I began lecturing together at colleges and universities across the United States. During one of our tours, we found ourselves with a day off in South Carolina, so we decided to visit some of the places where we had grown up.

One of the locations we visited was the former gas station that had been owned by my great-grandfather in a small town just outside Spartanburg. When I pointed out the old building to Patti, she looked at me wide-eyed and said, "No freakin' way!" I asked her what she meant and she told me that when she was a little girl, she had ridden her bicycle to that very gas station to buy soft drinks and candy from the little old man who owned the place. That little old man, it turned out, was my mother's father's father!

Patti and I both shook our heads in amazement and talked for quite a while about how our lives had almost intersected so many years before we finally met!

In 2005, Patti and I appeared together on an episode of the TV show *Airline*. A film crew followed us on an investigation of Sloss Furnaces, a reputedly haunted former iron mill located in Birmingham, Alabama. This was my first international television exposure as a psychic and medium.

Then, in January of 2007, I was asked to appear as a guest psychic on an upcoming show called *Paranormal U* (one of the titles originally considered for the hit TV series *Paranormal State*) that was being produced for the A&E network. The show was about a group of students from Penn State University who had formed a campus organization called the Paranormal Research Society, or PRS, that was dedicated to researching and investigating all things paranormal. Prior to the show's leaving the air in 2011, I appeared on thirty-one episodes of *Paranormal State*.

In March of 2007, I went to Las Vegas to film one of those episodes. As always, I knew nothing about the case we would be investigating. The production staff went to great lengths to keep me completely uninformed. In fact we often joked that it was as if I were being quarantined and kept in isolation. The subject of this particular episode turned out to be a teenager named Savannah who was being visited by the ghost of a girl who had been murdered in Texas. Over the course of filming during the next couple of days, I spent a lot of time with Savannah, counseling her about her psychic abilities and calming her fears and doubts.

A few days after I returned home, I received a phone call from Betsy Schechter at Four Seasons Productions (now Picture Shack Entertainment), one of the executive producers of the show. Betsy had been aware of me and my work for quite some time, even prior to my first appearance on *Paranormal State*, and had expressed interest in developing a television project with me. She told me that she and other producers had been very impressed by the way I worked with Savannah and asked me if I would be interested in working on a documentary about helping psychic kids and their families as I had done with Savannah and her mom in Las Vegas. Would I be interested? You bet!

Later that year, we filmed the *Psychic Kids* documentary at a remote sleepaway camp in Massachusetts where we had very limited telephone and Internet services. We were pretty much cut off from the rest of the world.

I knew from the beginning that what we were doing would be both groundbreaking and controversial. I knew there were children with psychic abilities who needed guidance and direction in order to cope with and manage their abilities. I also knew that there would be naysayers who would surely view these children as attention seekers and/or psychologically damaged.

As a psychic and medium, I had already been subjected to the nasty comments some people make about me and my profession. Now I was running the very real risk of being accused of indulging and exploiting children. But I couldn't let that possibility prevent me from doing what I knew was good and important work.

Quickly, it became very evident that most of these children and their families were in crisis mode. They had reached the end of their rope and they needed help. I was pleased to discover that the producers had assembled a team of professionals, including Dr. Lisa Miller, a licensed psychologist from Columbia University, to work alongside me on the documentary.

For three days, we spent countless hours working with the kids and their parents, but we also had fun during our downtime, sharing meals, chatting late at night beside the roaring fireplace, and playing in the snow. Yes, it snowed while we were filming and the kids loved it, especially Cooper, a boy you will meet later in this book, because it was the very first time he had ever seen snow.

By the time I left for home, I could see the many positive changes we had made in the lives of the children and their families. I felt very pleased and satisfied.

When the documentary aired, it was a huge hit. Audiences loved it, so the A&E network decided to turn *Psychic Kids* into a regular series. The producers began looking for other children and families who needed help. Much to everyone's surprise, we didn't need to look very far; we were receiving thousands of requests. The following spring, we began filming the first season of *Psychic Kids*.

Since then, we have completed two additional seasons of *Psychic Kids* and the series has aired on television all around the world. I have also appeared on CNN's *Larry King Live*, ABC's *Good Morning America*, and on the syndicated television show *The Tyra Banks Show*, featuring host Tyra Banks. I feel immensely blessed to be doing the work that I am doing, and now more than a decade after leaving the travel industry behind (or its leaving me), I'm still keeping myself—along with my dogs, my cat, and my cousin Kenny, who all live with me—housed and well fed.

In the chapters that follow you'll be meeting many of the psychic kids with whom I've worked over the years and also hearing more about my own personal growth and psychic development. It is my sincere hope that by the time you're done you'll have a better understanding of what "growing up psychic" really means.

CHAPTER ONE

What Does "Psychic" Really Mean?

First and foremost, I'd like to conclusively demystify what the terms "psychic" and "paranormal" actually mean. "Para," from the Greek for "beside," has also come to mean "beyond," and "paranormal" is a term now generally used to define experiences that are beyond the range of normal human experience. Or, as I like to say: Can't understand it. Can't explain it. But also can't deny that something is definitely going on here.

Within the realm of the paranormal there are absolutely no absolutes. Although there is currently a great deal of research being conducted in the field and much compelling evidence for the survival of the soul after death, nothing has yet been absolutely proved or disproved.

To describe someone as psychic is simply to say that he or she has a heightened ability to experience paranormal phenomena. Many people equate the term "psychic" either with something weird or with a phony sideshow fortune-teller at a carnival sitting in a dark, smoky tent wearing a turban and gazing into a crystal ball. But there's nothing weird or phony about psychic kids, and they certainly don't look any different from their peers.

In reality, being psychic is simply having the ability to pull in energy and receive information that cannot be accessed using the five human senses. How does this strange phenomenon occur? I have absolutely no idea, but it does. Quite often when I give people valid psychic information, they want to know, "How did you know that?" I just shrug my shoulders, shake my head, and tell them, "I don't know how I know what I know, I just know that I know it." And it's precisely the same for other psychics.

I believe that everyone is psychic to some degree; we all get hunches or gut feelings, and we all depend upon our intuition to make decisions at one time or another. People with psychic gifts are simply better able than most to tap into those nonrational sources of knowledge that exist in the world of spirit.

Consider, for example, how often you've thought of a friend or a loved one with whom you've lost contact, only to have him or her call you on the phone or send you an e-mail or even show up in person shortly afterward. What's happening is that you're sending the energy of your thought out into the universe and the connection is being reestablished.

Or have you thought of or talked about someone only to discover afterward that something significant happened to that person at just about the same time? If so, think about this: What are the chances of that being a coincidence? What are the Vegas odds of that happening?

These are just a few examples of the variety of psychic experiences we've all had, even if we don't recognize them as such. But there are many different kinds and degrees of psychic ability, and even the most gifted psychics are generally not equally adept at all of them.

THE MANY VARIETIES OF PSYCHIC ABILITY

Some, but not all, psychics are mediums, meaning that they have the ability to communicate with dead people. Some are gifted in precognition, crime solving, psychic healing or diagnosis, being empathic (sensing another person's physical or psychological problem even if he or she isn't aware of it), or communicating with animals. Over the years, I've encountered children—and adults—who are gifted in every one of these areas.

WHEN GLADYS PRESLEY CAME CALLING

Back in 1977 my mother had a curious and inexplicable experience. She was lying in bed one night when a woman appeared and began speaking to her. The woman, whom my mother recognized from newspaper and magazine photos as Elvis Presley's beloved mother, Gladys (who had died in 1958), said that she needed my mother's help because if someone didn't do something, her son was going to die of a drug overdose in the bathroom of his home in seven days.

When my mother told me about her visitation the next morning, we both had the same questions: Why on earth would Gladys Presley come to her? Why would she think my mother could do anything to help her? We had no idea. And we also didn't know whether Mrs. Presley had visited other people or whether my mother had, for some reason, been singled out. We were confused, and my mother, who was an Elvis fan, was very troubled. She did try to reach out to some of the people who were close to the King, but no one took her seriously, and sure enough, much to our amazement, seven days later, on August 16, 1977, we heard on the radio that he had died of a drug overdose in the bathroom at Graceland.

I still sometimes wonder whether there was anything anyone could have done to prevent Elvis's death that day. Was it his soul's evolution? Was there any way to have changed that path? It's something I'll never know.

I didn't discover my own gift for mediumship until I was well into my forties. Even though I'd been psychic my entire life, as a medium I was a late bloomer, and I truly believe that this particular ability manifested itself at the point in my life where I was ready to accept it. I was working in the travel industry and one of my coworkers, a woman

I'll call Pat, had had an older brother who had been in a car accident and died many years ago. One Friday after work Pat told me that she was going to do some shopping at one of the big discount clubs and asked me if I'd like to come along and grab a bite to eat afterward. We each took our own car and then wandered the aisles together examining everything from electric saws to giant jars of mayonnaise. As we were about to leave I stopped to look at the small section of books on display. When I picked up one by renowned psychic and medium John Edward, Pat began to sing his praises, telling me that she'd seen him on TV and raving about how great he was. I put the book down, started to walk away, and then went back and put it in my cart. Later, at home, I started to read it and didn't put it down until I'd finished the whole thing in one sitting.

Fast-forward to the following Friday when Pat and I again met in the parking deck. As we stood chatting by our cars I suddenly heard a voice in my head saying, "Tell Pat hello from me." I had no idea what was going on. In fact, I was a bit freaked out, so I decided to ignore it. But the voice wouldn't go away. A few seconds later I heard it again. "Tell Pat hello from me," this time more insistently. Reluctantly, I told Pat what was happening. I thought she'd think I was going nuts, but instead she just looked at me and said, "Who is it?" I shrugged, and then, in the next instant, I sensed that it was a young male and I knew that his name began with the letter T. I told this to Pat and, without really thinking about it, added, "His name is something like Tony or Tommy or Terry."

"My brother's name was Tony," Pat said. "Do you think he's trying to talk to me through you? Is he saying anything else?" At that point it was as if the floodgates had opened and I began to receive messages so rapidly that I couldn't keep up with what was coming to me.

"He says he didn't die in the car wreck," I told her, and she confirmed that this was true. I began to feel a tremendous pressure inside my head and then a popping sensation, as if a balloon had burst. When I reported this to Pat she said that her brother had suffered a brain aneurysm while driving and that's what had caused him to crash the car.

"He's showing me the number six," I said. "Did he live for six hours or six days or six weeks after the accident?"

"Six weeks," she said somberly.

I continued to receive other messages from Tony, including the fact that he took Pat out for ice cream the night before the accident and that he knew Pat had visited him in the intensive care unit of the hospital the night before he died, when another aneurysm had ruptured in his brain.

"There's no way he could've known that I was there," she said. "He was in a coma."

"He says his eyes were open," I told her.

"They were closed!" she said, almost angrily.

"He says he saw you and he wants you to know that it didn't hurt."

Pat began to cry. "It did hurt," she sobbed bitterly. "He had tears in his eyes!"

"Tell her I said, 'It didn't hurt, you little shit!'" Tony said to me. Reluctantly, I relayed the message to Pat, and she gasped audibly.

"That's what he always used to call me when he was angry at me. He called me 'you little shit!'" she said.

Pat seemed overwhelmed by what was happening, wanting to believe, yet doubtful. "If he really is talking to you, if he really knew I was at the hospital the night before he died, ask him to tell you what I was wearing."

I've discovered over the years that spirits seldom like being challenged to provide "proof" that they are really communicating, but Tony did not back down from the challenge. Immediately, inside my mind, I found myself in an Italian restaurant. I could see the dark wood-paneled walls and the tables and chairs. "I'm seeing red and white . . . checkered . . . gingham . . . like tablecloths in an Italian restaurant."

Pat looked like she was going to faint. "Oh, my God!" she said. "I was wearing a dress with a red and white checkered print near the collar when I visited him on the night before he died! There's no way you could've known that!" she said to me.

And so began my dialogues with the dead. Until that point the only interdimensional communication I'd had was at my father's funeral. I was sitting in the front row with my father's flag-draped closed coffin in front of me when, during the sermon, I closed my eyes and then suddenly I saw Dad standing in front of me. He'd had a leg amputated and for the first time in three years, there he stood on two feet. Speaking into my inner ear, he said, "Promise me that you will always take care of your mother." I sent him a silent message saying, "You know I will," and with that he was gone. And that was it—until Pat and Tony.

Since then I have reconnected thousands of people with their loved ones who have passed away, and I have had the good fortune to deliver many healing—even lifesaving—messages from those in spirit.

WHEN GUILT BECOMES OVERWHELMING

Several years ago, I received an urgent phone call from Sylvia, a fellow psychic for whom mediumship was not a forte. Sylvia asked me to come immediately to consult on a very serious case that was truly a matter of life and death. I hopped in my car and drove to her home, where I met sixteen-year-old Cindy and her lovely but totally distraught mother, Linda.

It was obvious that Cindy had been crying, and Sylvia explained that she had recently suffered a devastating loss and needed to communicate with a deceased loved one. As I always do, I asked only for the name of the person Cindy wished to contact, the relationship she'd had with the individual, and how long it had been since he died.

"His name was Rob, he was my boyfriend, and he died a couple of months ago," Cindy said in a quavering voice.

I quickly made contact with Rob's spirit and knew immediately that he had died unexpectedly and tragically. One of the first things he said to me was, "Tell Cindy it's not her fault." When I relayed that message both Cindy and her mom began to sob uncontrollably.

Over the course of the next hour, Rob delivered numerous messages about the time he and Cindy had spent together. Gradually I felt my connection with him begin to fade, but before he left he wanted me to once again tell Cindy very firmly that what had happened to him was not her fault. At the end of the reading, both Cindy and her mom looked as if they'd been relieved of a huge burden.

As I found out, Cindy and Rob had been high school sweethearts. They went to the prom together and shared a sweet romance. Sadly, however, other aspects of Rob's life were far from sweet. His parents had recently gone through a bitter divorce, and he and his mom had been living in the basement apartment of her parents' home. Rob was angry and depressed.

One night when he and Cindy were at a party, she accused him of flirting with another girl. Rob had been drinking, tempers flared, and they had a nasty argument. Cindy left the party alone and went home. Although Rob tried to call her on her cell phone several times, she refused to answer his calls. The last time he called he left a voice mail message for her saying, "What I am going to do is your fault."

That night, Rob hanged himself in the shower of his grandparents' basement apartment. Cindy was understandably devastated and blamed herself. After all, she had refused to take his calls and he had told her in his final message that his death was her fault. By the time I met her, she was so upset and guilt ridden that she was contemplating taking her own life.

She was in therapy, and I urged her to continue the process. There was a history of suicide in the family, and I was seriously worried about Cindy. Firmly but lovingly, I told her that suicide was not the answer to her problems, and I made her swear to me that she would never try to take her own life.

I've remained in contact with Cindy and her family throughout the years and am happy to say that she has graduated college and is now a happy and healthy young woman. Cindy recently sent an e-mail to me that included the following: "Chip, I want to thank you for all that you did for me. I don't know if I could have made it through Rob's suicide without you. You are a true angel."

Having recently read that suicide is the third leading cause of death in young people aged fifteen through twenty-four, I am very grateful that my being able to contact Rob all those years ago contributed to her recovery from guilt and depression.

But, as I've said, mediumship is only one of the many varieties of psychic ability. Twelve-year-old Brad C. and his ten-year-old sister, Morgan, who appeared on the very first episode of *Psychic Kids*, were both psychic. Their parents both work in alternative health care—their father a chiropractor and their mother a Reiki master—and both were highly accepting and supportive of their children's abilities, but Brad was, nevertheless, not quite comfortable with his gift. Morgan, on the other hand, was extremely well-adjusted and curious about paranormal phenomena, as well as very proud of her psychic abilities.

The only disturbing aspect of her gift was that she sometimes received extremely accurate precognitive flashes of disasters that had not yet occurred, including, most notably for me, "seeing" a clear picture of large numbers of people being drowned before the tsunami in Indonesia. She wasn't sure why she was getting this information or what, if anything, she was supposed to be doing with it, and that was upsetting to her.

I'm sure we've all received gifts we wouldn't have chosen for ourselves, but unlike the ugly sweater you may have received from your aunt Rita, precognition is not something you can simply regift or donate to Goodwill. Receiving information from a source that can't be explained rationally always puts one in an awkward (to say the least) situation. What are you supposed to do with that information? Do you call the authorities? What if they think you're crazy? What if you're wrong? Many adults agonize over these questions, so imagine how disturbing they would be for a young child.

I couldn't tell Morgan why she was receiving this information; no one really knows why some people are gifted with precognition. But I suggested that one thing she could do would be to send out positive energy, pray for the people who might be affected, and to do whatever she could energetically to possibly mitigate the seriousness of the situation. As the child of alternative medical practitioners, Morgan was aware of how healing the flow of energy can be, and the idea that she could send her own positive energy out into the world was extremely empowering for her.

Recently, I spoke with Brad and Morgan's mom, Marsha, for the first time in a couple of years and was very pleased to learn that both kids are doing well. Brad is playing lacrosse, is thinking about pursuing media studies, and has decided to try his hand at stand-up comedy. His mom says that he is "a bright, confident, funny man who squeezes every drop of hilarity out of his day." Morgan, who is turning fourteen, has discovered dance and will soon be appearing in her first recital. She also enjoys playing the piano, photography, and especially her twenty-pound tabby cat. Mom says that she "is a compassionate, intelligent, and articulate young lady who spreads joy wherever she goes."

They are both very well-adjusted psychic kids!

COLT SPEAKS

Although I haven't actually met Colt, the story his mother, Angela, told me speaks to the issue of how important it is for parents to be supportive of their children's precognitive abilities.

Angela is the founder of Colts Camelot, a program that offers equine-related activities to children with disabilities so that they may improve their quality of life by achieving a variety of therapeutic goals—cognitive, physical, emotional, social, educational, and behavioral. Currently, she is also a stay-at-home mom who homeschools her two autistic sons and her daughter.

During her own childhood, Angela had numerous paranormal experiences. She says that because of her psychic abilities, she was often bullied, told that she had an overactive imagination, and warned never to speak openly about the strange occurrences that happened to her.

Years ago, when Colt was just eleven months old and virtually nonverbal (at least a year before his autism diagnosis), Angela was driving home with him from a family vacation to Gulf Shores, Alabama. Suddenly, Colt began to yell and cry from the backseat of the car. "Bad men on the plane! Buildings going to fall! Many people hurt! Help them!" he shouted. Angela was stunned, to say the least.

She pulled the car off to the side of the highway, shaken by what had just occurred. Colt was still upset, so she turned on the radio, hoping to find some music that would calm her son down. It was then that she heard the breaking news that the first airplane had hit one of the towers of the World Trade Center in New York City.

Since then Angela has discovered that she and Colt are often able to communicate nonverbally by sending each other telepathic messages. She has also learned that Colt often knows things that are going to happen before they actually occur. And she has been told by her aunt that many people throughout many generations within their family have had psychic abilities.

Colt is now almost eleven years old, and Angela describes him as being "very sensitive to both people and animals. He often senses the feelings, emotions, and pain of others and regularly knows about things that have happened when he wasn't present to witness them."

Angela's younger son, Morgan, who is also autistic, appears to have paranormal abilities as well. She says that she and Colt help Morgan to overcome the hurdles of autism and understand his own psychic gifts.

Another type of paranormal knowledge is psychic crime-solving. Several of the children on *Psychic Kids* have proved to be gifted psychic detectives (also known as forensic psychics), but, as with any kind of criminal investigation, there can be safety issues involved. One of the reasons you may not have heard about a psychic' having solved a crime is that law enforcement doesn't always make that information public. The authorities may simply be reluctant to admit that it's possible, or they may be protecting the person who provided the information.

Empaths are those who sense the emotions or psychological

feelings of others. They may also feel the residual imprint of emotions surrounding certain locations or left behind on objects. Often, when an empath walks into a room, he or she can sense what has taken place there. He may sense that there has been discord or suffering or disease in the room or that a person who was overbearing or grieving or in some kind of distress has been there. Many empaths are also gifted at psychic diagnosis—also called somatic intuition—and are able to feel and determine the source of other people's physical problems. They do this by accessing another person's body energy and somehow (remember, paranormal information is defined by the fact that it isn't subject to logical explanation) pinpointing the source of their sickness and pain.

Some empaths will actually walk into a room where someone has a headache and immediately take on that headache. To live comfortably with these abilities you need to be able to protect yourself from taking on other people's negative energy. In chapter 3 we'll be talking more about why it's so important for psychic kids to take control of and manage their abilities. For now, however, I just want to point out that feeling other people's pain would be burdensome to anyone, but to a child who hasn't yet learned to take command of it, this particular "gift" can become overwhelming.

And, finally, there are those who have the ability to communicate with animals. One of the most gifted animal communicators I've ever met is Alexandra Breed, who appeared on *Psychic Kids* when she was still in high school. On the program, she was able to correctly diagnose a dog's mysterious medical problems and give that information to the owner. Now a college student, Alexandra is already a nationally recognized animal communicator who works extensively with Atlanta-based Angels Among Us Pet Rescue, often appearing at its fundraising events.

EVEN PSYCHICS DON'T KNOW EVERYTHING

So, as we've seen, being psychic is not an all-or-nothing proposition, even though many people—most of them skeptics—seem to think it should be. Some time ago, one skeptic with whom I'd had many previous run-ins informed me that he'd bought tickets to one of my events. Knowing how disruptive his presence would be, I informed him that he wasn't welcome and insisted on refunding his money. I'd already checked to see that no tickets had been purchased in his name, so I asked him to tell me what name he had used to buy them. At that point he laughed and said, "Ha ha, I didn't actually purchase any tickets and if you were really psychic you would have known that." Of course, he was being ridiculous—as ridiculous as all those people who keep asking me why, if I'm so psychic, I don't know the winning lottery numbers. My answer to these naysayers is always the same: No psychic knows everything; that's God's job. Omniscience is a divine power, not a psychic power, and while I believe that my abilities come from a divine place, neither I nor any other psychic I know would ever claim to have divine power. In fact, what that sneaky skeptic actually proved was not that he could trick me or that I wasn't psychic. All he really proved was that he is a liar.

And, furthermore, because psychic information results from an interdimensional transfer of energy, the intent of the seeker impacts the result. When I'm doing an event before a live audience, for example, the intent of the people in the room significantly affects what I am able to pull in. If I'm in a room full of people who are intent on having communication, it will happen. If I'm in a room full of people who are tired, who've been drinking, or who are not serious about what they're doing, the vibration will be off and the response will be weak or discordant. If there's discord in the energy, it will negatively affect the results.

As I keep reminding the children I work with, having psychic gifts doesn't make them omniscient or omnipotent (personally, I wouldn't want that kind of power for myself), and it doesn't give them the ability to change another person's path. Sometimes it is possible to ease another person's pain by giving him or her a message from the world of spirit, but sometimes the recipient of the information may choose not to act on it or may be unable to change his soul path.

There's a phrase I've admittedly appropriated from the well-known psychic and medium John Holland because it reminds me when I sometimes forget that my job is only to deliver the message. The phrase is, "Through me, not for me." What this means to me is that once I've delivered the message my job is done. I cannot control, nor am I responsible for, what the recipient chooses to do with the information. What he does with what you give has nothing to do with you. I was reminded of this again very recently when I received a call from another psychic who had become obsessed with needing to know what his clients had done with the information he'd given them. He just couldn't let go of thinking that he somehow had to know the outcome. All I could tell him was that the outcome was none of his business. His only business was to deliver the message. And, in truth, the same holds true for any kind of advice or guidance you might give to anyone. You can tell anyone, with the best of intentions, what you believe would be best for her, but that's all you can do—you can't *make* anyone act on what you tell her.

This is a very important concept for psychic children to understand, particularly because these young people do take their gift very seriously and sometimes find it hard to let go of the message once it's been received and delivered.

HOW WE RECEIVE AND INTERPRET PSYCHIC INFORMATION

Paranormal information is being transferred from the spiritual plane, but we as humans receive and/or interpret that information by using our physical senses, and different senses may be more or less acute in different people. What this means is that some psychics "hear" the information, some "see" it physically or with their mind's eye, some "feel" it in their bodies, and others receive it as a kind of intellectual knowing, even if they don't know how or why they come to know what they know.

Joel, for example, was a lanky, athletic blond teenager whose parents had been divorced and who was living in a rather isolated, rural area in California. When I met him, Joel was confused and terrified because he was seeing all kinds of apparitions, including what he described as a white dog or a white wolf roaming the property of his ancestral home. He was also very closed off and reluctant to talk about what he'd been experiencing. I think he really believed that he was going crazy, but, thankfully, we were able to make him understand that even though he may have been emotionally affected by his family situation, that didn't mean he wasn't also receiving paranormal information—and it certainly didn't mean that he was mentally ill. To help him validate those experiences to himself, we gave him various kinds of equipment used in paranormal investigation, including an EMF (electromagnetic field) meter and a laser thermometer, and that's when he really started to open up—not only to us but also to the truth of what he'd been seeing and feeling. Suddenly he was able to view himself as a paranormal investigator, and that put him back in control of his own life.

MICHELLE GRIFFIN EXPLAINS PARANORMAL INVESTIGATIVE TOOLS

Michelle Griffin is a psychic who has been investigating claims of paranormal activity for more than a decade. Good investigators, she says, need to be both critical thinkers and healthy skeptics because "if we can rule out all explainable causes of alleged paranormal activity, we are better able to substantiate that the claim is, indeed, paranormal."

In season 2 of *Psychic Kids* Michelle worked on an episode with three teenage girls, demonstrating how certain instruments can be used to help validate people's psychic impressions of the world in which we live. The following is Michelle's advice on how parents can use these instruments to corroborate their child's claims.

While it is important to mention that to date there is no completely irrefutable proof of ghosts, spirits, psychic abilities, etc., it is equally important to note that there is substantive evidence of these phenomena that continues to remain unexplainable. There are some great, easily obtainable, and even inexpensive devices that can be used. Following is a brief introduction to the ones that are used most frequently.

Audio recorders are typically used to record electronic voice phenomena (EVPs), which are "voices"—and sometimes other sounds—that are generally not detected by the human ear and can be heard only during playback. One explanation that has been suggested for this is that spirit voices are not within the range of human hearing. These voices often have certain similar characteristics. They tend to be whispers or have a lilting or singsong quality and may require several attempts to decipher. Occasionally, however, an EVP is so distinct and clear it's surprising the investigators didn't hear it at the time it was recorded. EVPs are arguably the most compelling evidence of the existence of ghosts and spirits.

The vast majority of investigators use digital voice recorders, ranging in price from inexpensive to very costly. Some investigators prefer specific brands, but any one will work just fine. You might want to choose a model that allows you to transfer your recordings to a computer via a USB connection.

If you already have an analog tape recorder, you can use that, too. Just be sure to use a clean, unused tape each time you record in order to prevent possible bleed-through from previous recordings.

Here are a few pointers for conducting an EVP session:

- If you choose to ask questions aloud, leave enough time for a response before continuing.
- Keep background noise to a minimum and, as you are recording, state into the machine any background sounds you may hear. (A dog barking in the distance, for example, can sound quite different when you listen back later and forget that you heard it.) Make sure no one whispers, as this could be hard to differentiate from an actual EVP.
- Keep recording sessions short. It can be tedious to listen to an hour of recording, and you can easily lose your focus. It is generally better to conduct several short sessions.
- Do not use the voice activation feature of your recorder.

Some investigators leave their recorder in an empty room set to record only if there is a voice or other noise. The problem with this is that the first part of the EVP can be lost because of the slight delay between voice activation and the beginning of the recording.

- Try to listen to your recordings immediately after each session. If you happen to record a voice or a reply to a question, you may then start another session, directing your questions accordingly.

- For optimal results, use headphones when reviewing your sessions. As I've said, EVPs can be difficult to hear and may even be obscured behind other noises, including your own voice. Make sure you are in a quiet environment during playback.

EMF (electromagnetic field) meters: A wide variety of these are available for use during paranormal investigations. Everything—including humans—has an energetic, electromagnetic field around it. The strength of this field varies from object to object. Being able to detect changes in EMF can tell you many things about the activity taking place throughout a particular location.

Many people believe that the presence of spirit energy causes a disturbance in the EMF. We have all heard unexplainable stories of televisions turning on or off, lights flickering, etc., all of which may possibly be examples of spirit energy disturbances. It is also widely believed that spirits acquire energy from surrounding energy sources, such as batteries in cameras and audio or video recorders, in order to manifest themselves.

Once you begin an investigation, you should always conduct

an "EMF sweep," making note of the EMF readings in each area you are investigating in order to establish a baseline reading. If nothing changes in the environment, the EMF readings should remain the same. Using meters allows you to detect subtle EMF changes, and if there is no rational explanation for these changes, you may be detecting the paranormal presence of spirit energy. This can help to corroborate information that is being received by a psychic who is sensing spirit energy, as occurred several times when I was working with the young girls on *Psychic Kids*.

It should also be noted, however, that an extremely high EMF is capable of causing hallucinations. I remember being called to the home of an elderly woman who described an entity that, she said, would enter through the ceiling of her bedroom as she lay in bed at night. She was becoming increasingly frightened and disturbed, and her daughter had taken her to several different doctors who could find no medical explanation for what she was experiencing. When my team and I entered her bedroom, we took EMF readings from all areas and discovered an incredibly high EMF surrounding an antique alarm clock on her nightstand that was emanating out and over her bed. We suggested that she remove the alarm clock from the bedroom, and when she did, the "activity" stopped. From that we determined that the clock's EMF was causing her to imagine that something paranormal was occurring when, in fact, it was not.

Cameras: Many different types are used during paranormal investigations: Digital (still photography) cameras and video cameras are the most popular. Every investigator hopes to capture an undeniable, irrefutable image or video clip of a ghost.

If you've watched the popular paranormal shows on TV, you've undoubtedly seen some of the more costly camera equipment being used. Infrared surveillance systems are a great way to monitor rooms while you watch what's happening on video monitors. FLIR cameras allow you to see a visual representation of temperature, showing both cold and hot spots, and, if you are lucky, the outline of a ghost! Full-spectrum cameras see light in the ultraviolet (UV) and infrared (IR) ranges, the parts of the light spectrum that are beyond what the human eye can see. It is theorized that ghosts and spirits may be more visible in that range. But you don't actually need such expensive equipment to conduct a thorough investigation.

Visual phenomena called orbs often appear in still photos or videos as round, bubblelike objects that may be either clear or one of many colors. Many people get excited when they find an orb in their photo or video because they think they have captured an image of spirit energy. In reality, however, 99.9 percent of orb imagery is caused by environmental contaminants, such as dust or flying insects. To prove this for yourself, take a piece of toilet paper, ruffle it up into the air, and then take a picture. What you will see is a "family reunion of orbs" (a.k.a. dust particles).

Laser thermometers: These are used by paranormal investigators to detect significant temperature changes that may possibly indicate the presence of spirit energy. As I mentioned earlier when discussing EMF, it is theorized that spirits require energy in order to manifest into the third dimension. Drawing heat from the surrounding environment, resulting in what is commonly referred to as a "cold spot," may possibly indicate a ghostly presence.

Instrumental trans-communication (ITC): This is a method of communicating with the spiritual plane through the use of electronic or mechanical devices. EVP is an example of this, but the term is more commonly used to describe the use of devices other than voice recorders, such as television sets, computers, telephones, and even fax machines.

On an episode of *Psychic Kids*, I used a device called a **Frank's Box**, an electronic device created by Frank Sumption in 2002 that allegedly allows real-time communication with other dimensions, including the spirit realm. The device is a combination of a white noise generator and a radio receiver that has been modified to continuously sweep back and forth through radio bands, selecting snippets of sound to create what may be heard as messages from disincarnate entities.

Another ITC device that many investigators use is the **Ovilus**, created by electronics engineer Bill Chappell. The Ovilus contains a database of words and an EMF detector that work in tandem to generate what some consider to be messages from disincarnate beings.

Although devices like these have been used for decades, they remain highly controversial because of our brain's natural inclination to try to make logical sense of all sounds. Newer and different versions of these types of audio communication tools are being developed by a number of people.

As Michelle has said, the use of these instruments may provide positive indications that a psychic kid's impressions are on the right track. But she adds, "As a former psychic kid and current mom to children who have had paranormal experiences, I strongly advise you to listen closely to your children when they speak about matters pertaining to the paranormal, regardless of the results you may get when using investigative equipment."

While the majority of children I've worked with talk about seeing spirits, others say that they *feel* spirit energy in an otherwise empty room, and we've already talked about the fact that empaths feel other people's pain. When we talk about a spirit energy telling us something, it's not the same thing as hearing voices. Rather it's that we have no other way to describe the way we're receiving this information than to equate it with one of the five human senses. For me, the information feels somehow alien inside my head, as if it doesn't belong to me. It's just there, as if it had come out of nowhere, and many times, before I can even develop it into a conscious thought, it's coming out of my mouth, almost like an involuntary reflex. We blink our eyes millions of times a day without ever thinking about what we're doing, and that's very similar to the way I receive and deliver paranormal information.

So if an otherwise healthy child says he hears voices, or sees apparitions, or feels another person's pain, or knows when danger is approaching, he is describing a particular psychic phenomenon even if he doesn't quite have the words to define it.

CAN PEOPLE LEARN TO BE "MORE PSYCHIC"?

My own abilities came to me naturally and organically. Although I have had various teachers and mentors during my life, I never had to "develop" my abilities. However, that's not always the case.

"Can I learn to be more psychic?" "I had abilities as a child, but I shut them out. Can I get those abilities back?" Those are questions I've been asked thousands of times. My response is always "Maybe," because there are no guarantees or absolutes in the world of psychic phenomena.

Some people simply need to focus on and pay closer attention to their own intuition. They may be dismissing or discounting valid information they are receiving. Others find reading books or taking classes or watching DVDs about psychic development to be beneficial to them.

My friend Echo Bodine (yes, that's her real name) has taught psychic development for more than thirty years. As a young girl, Echo always seemed to "know" things, and at the age of seventeen, she was told by a psychic and medium that she, too, had these abilities, but they needed to be nourished. For more than a year, Echo studied with and took classes from a psychic and spiritualist minister.

She now teaches online psychic development classes, and her books *A Still, Small Voice* and *The Gift* are both great resources for those who are trying to understand and develop their psychic and intuitive abilities. "These are wonderful gifts, and we all have them, to one degree or another," Echo says. "They can be challenging at times and downright hard to deal with, but the more knowledge you have, the better you will be at navigating them."

Lots of "regular people" have taken Echo's classes. "I've taught Realtors who want to enhance their psychic abilities in order to find the perfect homes for their clients, medical professionals who want to use their abilities to work with patients, teachers who want to know how to better relate to their 'sensitive' students, as well as parents and grandparents who want to better understand their psychic kids or grandkids," she told me.

Echo also believes that it is possible to revive psychic abilities that have, for whatever reason, been placed "on hold." In her opinion, "it's like riding a bike. Psychic abilities will return if and when someone is ready to accept them and devote some time to [embracing] them."

CHAPTER TWO

So You Think Your Child Is Psychic

P arents who suspect or believe their child is psychic react in many different ways. Some are confused; some are frightened. Some are in a state of disbelief, and some are excited because they think their child is "special." Working with psychic kids both on camera and off, I've encountered every one of these responses. While there is no right or wrong response to discovering that you are the parent of a child who seems to have enhanced psychic abilities, some responses are more helpful than others—for both the parent and the child.

When she appeared on the television series *Psychic Kids,* redheaded Olivia K. was a bright, articulate, outgoing, but increasingly troubled seventeen-year-old high school student living in California with her mother, who was and is a down-to-earth, pragmatic, and practical woman. Although Olivia's mom never thought her daughter was making up the psychic experiences she described, she was still finding it hard to believe that Olivia was actually, as she put it, "seeing spirits."

She contacted the producers of *Psychic Kids* because she was uncertain about just what was going on and she wanted to learn more about what was happening to her child. Was Olivia K. really communicating with the world of spirit? Could her experiences actually be proven? Could she be in some kind of danger? Olivia's mom was a typical "show me" kind of person, and "show her" is exactly what we were able to do.

We filmed the program at an inn that was known to be occupied by spirits, and as I guided Olivia through the unoccupied rooms, her mother watched on our video monitors. She was amazed to see her daughter's reactions and hear the information Olivia seemed to be receiving, and when I explained to her that Olivia was sensing exactly what we had previously been told about the inn's former occupants and what had happened to them there, she was finally able to accept the validity of what her daughter had been telling her all along. I'm delighted to report that Olivia K. is now thriving, and her mother has become not only a firm believer in the paranormal but also her daughter's strongest supporter.

IN HER OWN WORDS: WHERE OLIVIA K. IS NOW

Being on *Psychic Kids* definitely changed my life. I am much more confident in myself now, more than ever before. I have control over my abilities and that has resulted in control over my life. If I could do it all over again, I would, in a heartbeat. I'm motivated and inspired to help other people my age who didn't have the opportunity to be on the show.

Life has been amazing. My grades have improved tremendously since filming *Psychic Kids*. I'll be a senior in high school this coming year and I'm looking forward to all that life has to offer. With no fear and no doubt, I'm going to set the world on fire!

And her mother adds:

"I became more open to the idea that I may be intuitive and I listen to my feelings more. Olivia shares more with me and we sometimes validate each other's 'sense' of a situation. I read Judith Orloff's book *Second Sight* and pay attention to my dreams more and try to get help from them.

"I have had four coworkers approach me about seeing the show. I have become more open and even more assertive. I am becoming more involved in the community. Again, I listen more to my feelings. I work in four different medical facilities as a family nurse practitioner, and I feel different in each one due to the overall personality or atmosphere in each place. I can feel so different, even from one patient's room to another."

IT'S A GIFT TO BE PSYCHIC

If a parent has never personally had a psychic experience (or at least is not aware of having had one, since most of us do at one time or another, whether we realize it or not), what he wants more than anything else is reassurance and information. The most important thing I can do to both inform and reassure him is to let him know that being psychic is a gift. It's a God-given ability just like being a piano prodigy or a math whiz or a budding tennis star. Just about anyone can learn to play the piano or hit a tennis ball over the net, and everyone has some degree of psychic ability. Psychic children, however, have a special talent for tapping into their "sixth sense" that needs to be protected and nurtured just like any other gift. All gifted children are "different" in some way, and they all need support and encouragement in order to thrive.

That said, it's also true that not all psychics (be they children or adults) are gifted in exactly the same way. Different people have different skill sets. Michael Jordan, for example, may have been the greatest basketball player ever, but he wasn't so great when he tried to play pro baseball. Some people can solve complicated math problems in their head, but they aren't necessarily brilliant writers. And, as we discussed in the previous chapter, some psychics may communicate with entities in the world of spirit while others are able to predict future events, and still others may be good at psychic crime-solving or communicating with animals. Some hear things, others see them, and some feel psychic energy in their bodies. Some are visited by only one particular spirit while others appear to be bombarded by a host of unwelcome visitors. With that in mind, it should be clear that it isn't really useful, and could be detrimental, to compare one child's abilities to those of another. If Johnny can do something Susie can't, it doesn't mean that Johnny is necessarily "more psychic" than Susie. If Johnny did great on his math SAT and Susie got a higher score in English, would that make one of them smarter than the other? No! It would just mean that they have different talents, and the same is true for psychic talent.

CHARLOTTE SCOTT ON THE IMPORTANCE OF EMPOWERING CHILDREN

Charlotte Scott is an amazing energy worker and one of the most spiritually connected people I have ever known. Energy work is closely related to various techniques used in ancient Eastern medicine, the most familiar of which are probably acupuncture and acupressure. The purpose is to unblock and release the flow of energy at various points in the body and to clear negative energy from physical spaces.

Charlotte is extremely attuned to the gifts of children that may not initially be visible to those who are too quick to define that child in terms of a medical, emotional, or psychological diagnosis and, therefore, fail to see abilities that are not so apparent.

Charlotte says:

As a child, I was not acknowledged as an empath or intuitive. I was judged harshly because of my abilities. Everyone tried to force me into the "normal box" and make me conform to their rules of life. My ability to sense things, my intuitive touch, and my massive curiosity for things that others considered "forbidden" were all squelched. And I did not respond well. It took me many years to understand that my unique perceptions of life are not always shared by those around me, that they cannot see or feel what I see and feel.

I discover more and more through my work with children that brilliance is often a condition of being born and living outside of the "normal box." Sometimes, they bring great levels of awareness but simply don't have the communication skills to convey it. Society calls these children everything from mentally challenged to autistic to genius and gives them labels like ADD and ADHD. Humans who are born outside the "normal box"— including psychic kids—get forced into categories.

For more than thirteen years I have worked with a young man named Josh, who was diagnosed as autistic. When I met Josh, he was a noncommunicative sixteen-year-old whose energy was considerably out of balance. Teenage hormones were raging inside his body, but his ability to process what was happening to him was only that of a seven-year-old child.

Josh had a very difficult and traumatic birth, including a period of oxygen deprivation, which became the medical explanation for his physical and mental problems. Fortunately, he has loving and supportive parents who understood that Josh could flourish if given the chance to do so.

During the many sessions I have had with Josh, he has readily slipped off into a meditative and healing space, connecting quickly with his higher self. All I ever need to do is facilitate the grounding and provide the space. Together, we have done a great deal of brain balancing, energy work, and past-life healing. The results have been nothing short of miraculous. Josh has so many amazing gifts! He did not come into this world without them; he came with an abundance of them. He just needed guidance and support to access and utilize them.

Today, Josh is twenty-nine years old and functioning quite well. He has a job at a school cafeteria and volunteers at the local aquarium, giving tours of the dolphin show and other special features of the facility. Josh is amazingly smart, literally a walking encyclopedia of information about all kinds of plants, animals, and insects. He is very in tune and familiar with nature, and his sensitivities open him up to a level of experience with the world around him that most of us simply don't understand.

Working with Josh helped me to realize that if we are given the chance to flourish, our soul will find its true purpose and potential.

While Charlotte is not saying that Josh is psychic, the point of her story is that categorizing a child—or anyone—in terms of what might be most obvious about him can prevent us from discovering talents or gifts that may be hidden beneath those symptoms. Instead of defining a person in terms of his limitations, we need to find a way to release those hidden talents and abilities—we need to dig beneath the surface to find that hidden richness.

Charlotte also works as a labor doula, assisting women during childbirth. "I see the foundation of life at the moment it begins to unfold," she says. "And I often find myself looking into a pair of eyes that hold ancient wisdom in a being that is only minutes old. It never escapes me that I am witnessing the moment when the world's population shifted plus one. The matrix has changed and this new being has purpose and intent. What might he or she do that would greatly impact the world?

It keeps me remembering that the cycle of life is constant and with every new life there is promise and hope. We are not born with just flesh and bone, but with a soul, a spirit, a greater self that manifests as the physical beings we are. And the possibilities are limitless!"

SO HOW CAN YOU REALLY KNOW?

I wish I could give you a checklist and simply say if you answer yes to six or more of these questions your child is definitely psychic. Unfortunately it's not that easy. There is no definitive guidebook to the paranormal; you can never really know exactly what to expect, and it may sometimes seem as if you're wading into a dark murky swamp and just hoping not to be bitten in the behind by an alligator. But just as you can test for math or English aptitude, there are also ways to validate psychic abilities. In fact, all the children who appear on *Psychic Kids* have been rigorously vetted, first by telephone and then by staff members who go to their homes and see how they and their families function. And even after they have been carefully evaluated and their experiences substantiated, they still have to prove themselves to me when we are filming.

While, in my experience, the vast majority of children who report having paranormal experiences really are psychic, there is always a slim possibility that they might simply have an overactive imagination or even some emotional, psychological, or neurological problem. I always assume a child's gift is real until proven otherwise, but I also think it's important to make sure there is no underlying health issue involved. That can be tricky, however, because traditional physicians or therapists might be influenced by their own preconceived ideas about psychic abilities and might, therefore, misdiagnose a psychic child as emotionally or mentally unstable.

EDY NATHAN TALKS ABOUT HELPING PSYCHIC KIDS

Edy Nathan is a licensed psychotherapist who was my cohost on seasons 2 and 3 of *Psychic Kids.* From the moment we met, it was apparent that we would work well together. I have a strong background in psychology and counseling, and Edy is very willing to think outside the clinical box. Although we didn't always agree on everything, we never failed to remember that our single goal was helping psychic kids and their families.

When I asked her why she is so willing to accept—when many others in the field of mental health are not—that some people have psychic and paranormal experiences, this was her response: "I have found a home with the beliefs of Dr. Carl Jung, an analyst who found a way to work with patients through their dreams, drawings, archetypes, and psychic experiences. He believed in a collective unconscious, a consciousness that goes far beyond the life we are currently living. It is these models that enable me to believe in the realm of psychic ability."

But she added, "It is often difficult to distinguish between a psychic experience and a psychological response to trauma. It is important to do a complete assessment of the child before you believe that he is psychic. Has he experienced trauma? What kind of trauma? Physical, emotional, and sexual abuse are certainly traumatic events that, if experienced by a child, should be dealt with in a professional setting with a therapist who specializes in the field of trauma and children. There are specific diagnostic tests that can be given to children to assess the level of trauma, if any, that they have experienced.

"You also want to make sure that there is nothing physically wrong with your child by having him evaluated by a medical professional."

And she cautioned, "After working in counseling for more than twenty years, I realize that therapists are often led by their fear of the unknown. If it does not fit into a diagnostic category, then it does not fit into their medical model of psychotherapy."

I wondered if Edy had found that others in her field are becoming more receptive to considering the validity of psychic and paranormal experiences, or whether she had suffered any backlash because of her own willingness to accept these phenomena.

"Others in my field are certainly becoming more open to alternative methods of therapy," she replied. "This, I believe, is opening the pathway for more receptivity to those with psychic ability. I have not suffered any backlash, primarily because I did not come into this field as a strict Freudian, but rather as a drama therapist. The therapists I have surrounded myself with are accepting of my desire to be in this field, working to define the relationship between the psyche and psychic ability.

"The techniques I use the most include cognitive behavioral therapy, hypnosis and guided imagery, play therapy, and role-play. Each of these techniques helps children who are scared and have lost their sense of self. They help them to become more self-confident and less dependent. It teaches them to learn to live their lives as seers in a positive and hopeful way. These techniques also promote healthy self-talk and personal motivation. The kids learn that when they step into their fear, it has less power over them."

I asked Edy one final question: Do you believe that professionals—medical doctors, mental health clinicians, educators, clergy, etc.—will ever accept the validity of psychic abilities and/or paranormal experiences?

"I hope so!" she responded. "In time—and with more proof, because the field is filled with pragmatists—I believe that there will be a change in perspective."

And I profoundly share that hope.

The story of Laura and her mother, Cheryl, illustrates how devastating a psychiatric misdiagnosis can be. Cheryl called me after seeing an episode of our program because Laura, who kept insisting that there was a ghost in her bedroom, had been clinically diagnosed as schizophrenic and put on antipsychotic medications. Cheryl was extremely upset because, after watching the program, she was becoming more and more convinced that the diagnosis was wrong. She also felt very guilty about having taken Laura to the psychiatrist in the first place. When we spoke, she told me that, except for seeing the ghost, Laura was a lovely, well-rounded twelve-year-old who didn't seem to have any other psychotic symptoms. It wasn't as if she were walking around claiming to hear voices telling her to do crazy things. Her spirit visitations were confined to her bedroom, where she frequently saw what she described as a pretty lady wearing old-fashioned clothing, who seemed very sad and appeared to be looking for something. But even though Cheryl couldn't believe that her daughter was, as she put it, "crazy," she was also finding it difficult to believe that Laura could actually communicate with the world of spirit—or that such a world even existed.

I explained to Cheryl that many mental health professionals are as skeptical as she was about the validity of something they can't understand on a rational level and that, for her own sanity as well as her daughter's, she needed to do some research to validate what Laura was telling her. I urged her to look up public records, go to the local library, and find out once and for all if there was any evidence to corroborate that the "pretty lady" had really existed.

The next time I heard from Cheryl she was very excited. She told me that she had taken my advice. She'd gone to the local town hall and gotten the names of the families who had previously occupied their house. Then she went to the library and started going through their newspaper archive. What she learned was that in the 1920s, the house had belonged to a young couple whose baby had died of SIDS in her crib, and that the mother was so distraught she had taken her own life not long after. Although Cheryl couldn't prove that Laura's bedroom was where the baby had died, she was now convinced that was the case and that the mother's spirit was still there, looking for her baby. Cheryl was almost in tears as she told me how deeply she regretted having doubted Laura and having allowed her to be put on medications she clearly didn't need.

Cheryl's story may sound extreme, but it's similar to stories I've heard over and over again. In fact, being afraid that their child could be stigmatized as mentally ill, put on medication, or even hospitalized is the reason many parents don't seek a professional evaluation.

And it's for that very reason that not only parents but also counselors, teachers, clergy, and health care providers need to be open-minded and educated about psychic phenomena and what psychic kids are receiving from the spirit world.

One woman who worked as a school counselor e-mailed to let me know that, although she herself had not encountered a psychic child in her practice, a colleague had told her about a young boy who reported having seen invisible people in the woods while he was riding the school bus. Her colleague was amused by the absurdity of his story and had chalked it up to the weird ramblings of a messed-up kid. She said that her colleague was very talented, but she had often thought about her attitude and wondered what had happened to that boy. "Your *Psychic Kids* show," she added, "has opened up my eyes to the difficulties faced by children with psychic abilities. Now if a child who saw spirits or communicated with the dead came into my office I would not be so quick to pass judgment on his sanity or the validity of his experiences." And she thanked me for helping her to "understand this misunderstood and often maligned segment of our population." Needless to say, I was extremely gratified to think that I had been able to play a role in opening the mind of even one educator.

It is fascinating—and unsettling—to me how far some clinicians will go to provide an explanation for what is clearly inexplicable. As one extreme example, while I was writing this I saw a report on a television news program about a woman who had undergone oral surgery and woke up from the anesthesia speaking with an Irish accent. The diagnosis? A rare condition called foreign accent syndrome. Now, I ask you, what does that really mean? Virtually nothing, and it certainly says nothing about what might have *caused* the condition.

In another, oddly similar situation, the mother of someone I knew many years ago had a serious stroke and was in a coma from which her doctors feared she would never awaken. Then one day her daughter received a call from the nursing home asking her to come over right away. Her mother hadn't died, they assured her, but they needed her to come. When she arrived, she was informed that her mother had come out of the coma—but she spoke and understood only French, a language she had never studied, understood, or spoken before! Then, after three days, the mother went to sleep one night and in the morning was speaking English again, with no memory of or explanation for what had occurred. The doctors at the nursing home couldn't explain it either, and in this case they didn't even try.

The point I want to make with these two stories is that sometimes things happen that simply can't be rationally or medically explained and that health care professionals need to accept that, because if they don't, they are likely to slap a diagnosis on a condition or phenomenon that is at best useless and at worst damaging to the individual who is labeled mentally or emotionally unstable.

Were these two women experiencing something from a past life? Had one of them been Irish and the other one French during a previous incarnation? I don't know. But what I do know is that their experiences exemplify my definition of paranormal: Can't understand it. Can't explain it. But also can't deny that something is definitely going on here.

Here's another example of the inexplicable things that occur in the world around us from my own personal experience. When I was a teenager and living in South Carolina, I was driving with my family to Florida—a ten- or twelve-hour trip at the time. To get there as quickly as possible, we were driving through the night, and my three much younger cousins were fast asleep in the car. We were somewhere in

Georgia when my four-year-old cousin, Michael, suddenly woke up, looked out the left-hand window, and said, "I used to live right over there." It was pitch-black outside. None of us could see a thing beyond the road, but even after we explained that we weren't anywhere near his home, Michael insisted that he had lived "right over there, in that yellow house on the other side of the railroad tracks." We assured him that he must have been dreaming and told him to go back to sleep, but when we passed the same location in broad daylight on the way home, sure enough, there were the tracks and the yellow house.

When I discussed the incident later with Michael's mother, it struck us that he may have been remembering a past-life experience, but, of course, we had no way to prove that.

If you believe that the soul survives physical death and continues to live on in the spirit realm, it is not a great stretch to believe our souls may also reincarnate and return to the physical world in another body. One instance in which reincarnation seems to be the only answer is the case of Vasur Patel. His aunt Nalini is a naturalized American citizen who grew up in India, where many of her family members continue to reside.

As a follower of the Hindu religion, Nalini believes in the concept of reincarnation, the process by which the soul of a once-living being returns to life in a new body or form, but she had not actually witnessed what she considered proof of reincarnation until her young nephew Vasur was about five years old and began speaking of his "other family," a wife and children living in another city in India, and citing events that occurred when he lived with them. The details that he provided were clear and precise and also quite convincing to Nalini.

For the next two years, Vasur begged his parents to take him to visit his "other family," and finally, they did. Together, they traveled to the distant city he had named, and Vasur led them directly to the house that he had described but had never visited during his current lifetime.

When they knocked on the door, a middle-aged woman answered and Vasur immediately embraced her, saying, "My wife, I have returned to you."

Imagine the woman's confusion and surprise! Vasur's parents explained his incredible story to the woman and she allowed them to come inside her home. As it turned out, she was a widow, and for the next several hours, Vasur provided her and her children with many accurate, personal details about the time when he had been her husband and their father.

To me, this is one of the most persuasive arguments in favor of reincarnation that I've ever heard. But again, the point is that when something inexplicable occurs we always want to know why. In medicine, this means providing a diagnosis. But some things just can't be explained.

SOME PSYCHIC KIDS DO HAVE OTHER PROBLEMS

All of the above notwithstanding, however, it's certainly possible that a psychic kid could also have psychological problems, which is why it's important for parents to have their children thoroughly evaluated by an appropriate, qualified health care provider. By "appropriate" I mean one who does *not* feel that he or she *must* find a rational, clinical diagnosis for what is occurring simply for the sake of making a diagnosis. This is particularly true when dealing with mental health providers. All too often they feel they must come up with a clinical explanation for everything and provide a diagnosis that fits within the parameters of the

Diagnostic and Statistical Manual, which has been called, and is generally accepted as, the bible for diagnosing mental illness.

I was recently reminded of one possible reason that so many therapists are so insistent on arriving at a clinical diagnosis, and, not surprisingly, it's directly related to problems with the health care system in America. A licensed professional counselor who has worked in the mental health field for many years wrote to say that even though she grew up in a family who strongly believe in the paranormal and in their own psychic gifts, "working with [psychic] kids is definitely a challenge in a pure clinical practice since this is not something you can bill insurance for." Her point is very valid. Medical and mental health professionals must provide a clinical—and billable—diagnosis in order to receive payment from insurance companies. It is frightening to imagine how many children have been misdiagnosed, mislabeled, and mistreated because of the need to satisfy insurance guidelines!

That said, however, even if a child truly is psychic, there may be some underlying or ancillary issue at work. In fact, a child who is having inexplicable psychic experiences may well be anxious, fearful, or depressed simply because he doesn't understand what's going on. But that does not in any way rule out the validity of his or her psychic abilities.

The important point here is that as a parent, you need to be completely honest and open both with any health care professional you consult and with yourself. Be honest about wanting to make certain that there isn't any mental or emotional problem involved and state that you do want your child to be thoroughly evaluated, but tell the doctor or therapist that you do not want to put your child on medication unless or until all other options have been ruled out. Make it clear that you don't want your child taking antidepressants or antipsychotic drugs unless it is absolutely necessary and that you don't want him to be labeled as mentally unhealthy. Then say, "I need to know if you're willing and able to work with me in this way."

If the answer is no, keep looking. If the answer is yes, you also need to tell the professional exactly what your child is experiencing, not only in terms of psychic phenomena but also in every other aspect of his life. Is there alcohol or drug abuse in your home? Is there any other type of chaos or dysfunction in your family? If you don't approach this in the spirit of full disclosure, you'll be cheating yourself, the health care provider, and, most important, your child.

WHEN PETER MET PABLO

Peter Davis Jr. is a mental health therapist who now resides in Oregon. In 2007, he was working for an organization in Southeast Idaho when he had an amazing encounter with a psychic child. Peter, who speaks English and Spanish, was visiting the home of a Mexican family when he met five-year-old Pablo.

When he walked into the small house, he "found everything to be quite normal." He recalls, "There were several kids running around, the smell of tortillas and beans filled the house, and the mother was kind and gracious. She had me sit at their small kitchen table and excused herself to check on a baby in another room."

It was then that a little boy came up and introduced himself to Peter. "He said his name was Pablo and he had something he needed to tell me. In Spanish, he said, 'Your grandma tells me to tell you hi.' My curiosity was piqued, so I asked Pablo to tell me the name of my grandmother, and he replied, 'Let me ask her.'"

At that point he turned and spoke to someone Peter couldn't see. Then he turned back and said, "She says her name is Wanda," which was, indeed, the name of Peter's deceased grandmother! Pablo delivered several messages from Wanda that were meaningful to Peter, including, "She remembers the time when you got sick from eating cotton candy at her house"—an occurrence that Peter, too, remembered very well.

Later, Peter mentioned to Pablo's mother what had happened. "The mother was very straightforward in telling me that Pablo was psychic and often talked with people who had passed on."

She also told Peter that Pablo's psychic abilities had frightened his teachers at Head Start, the government preschool program for low-income families that he attended, and that doctors had said, "Pablo has an overactive imagination and needs to watch less television."

Several years later, the incident with Pablo still stays in Peter's mind. "Pablo told me things that only my grandmother would know, things that a five-year-old boy would have no clue about."

Psychic kids are, first and foremost, kids. And just like every other kid who exists in the "real world," everything that happens to them has an impact on their physical and emotional health. When working with psychic kids and their families, I always look at the big picture rather than simply focusing solely on the child's abilities and paranormal experiences. Is their world a healthy, stable, and secure place? Or is it filled with discord and dysfunction? What is life like for them in the real world?

Those who are psychic are often called "sensitives," and psychic kids are generally hypersensitive to everything in the world around them. They tend to feel and sense things more acutely than kids who are not in tune with their psychic abilities. If left unchecked, this sensitivity can create a plethora of problems.

How you and your child cope with the child's being psychic may well depend on how well you both are coping with life as a whole. That's one of the reasons I always work with a therapist on *Psychic Kids* who can talk with the children and their parents about personal and family issues that may be affecting their lives. Providing a healthy, stable, and secure life for every child should always remain a top priority not only for parents but for everyone involved in the child's life.

I certainly don't want to frighten anyone, but I would be remiss if I did not advise that negative energies and entities are attracted to any environment that is filled with discord and dysfunction. And any psychic kid who lives in this type of environment is very likely to encounter those energies and entities, whose presence can further complicate an already stressful and unhealthy situation. We will talk specifically about psychic protection and how to deal with negative paranormal situations in chapter 4.

What you need to understand right now, however, is that just because a child has other issues affecting his life doesn't mean he's *not* psychic, any more than being psychic means he is mentally unbalanced.

DO YOUR OWN RESEARCH

Simply stated, the only way to determine if someone—a child or an adult—is receiving true psychic information is by confirming, validating, and corroborating that information. Otherwise, you will simply be left with a lot of huge question marks.

If you have ruled out the existence of other mental or emotional issues, there are many ways to validate psychic abilities that do not require professional help. If, for example, a child says that he's seeing a dead relative or some other individual whom he never knew in life, and if he actually identifies the person he is seeing by name or relationship (such as great-grandma), his ability to pick out that person from a "photo lineup" similar to those used by the police may be all the validation required.

Another way to validate the child's claims would be to corroborate what she's reporting through historical records as I suggested to Cheryl and as my mother and I did back in Elmira when we investigated the history of the Murphy house.

To give you another example of how to do this, Faith, an eight-year-old girl who appeared on *Psychic Kids*, reported that she was being visited by a boy named Freddie Stuart, who told her how old he was when he died and mentioned two particular women's names. To corroborate her experiences, we did our own extensive research—consulting the county historian at the library; looking through newspaper archives, property records, and death certificates; and searching online at ancestry.com—and we found that a boy named Freddie Stuart had indeed lived within eighty miles of the little girl, that he'd died at exactly the age she said he'd told her, and that the names he mentioned were those of his mother and the live-in housekeeper. There was no way Faith could have researched this information on her own.

She was not at all Internet savvy, and her parents attested to the fact that Faith had not done any research at the library or met with the county historian, as we did. We also found it highly unlikely that anyone had "fed" the information about Freddie Stuart and his family to Faith. So, what explanation could there be except that Freddie had truly come to her from the world of spirit?

There are many public records and historical resources available to anyone who is interested in using them and willing to put in the time and effort required. Yes, it may require a bit of research, but if that's what it takes to validate your child, reassure yourself, and confirm the existence of paranormal phenomena, it is certainly well worth it. Go to the town hall and research deeds to investigate the history of your home; research birth and death certificates; talk to the town historian at your local library; check old newspaper records. In many cases, if a person died young, died in an accident, or was murdered, or if there was any unusual event such as a house fire or a flood associated with the death, there will be a newspaper story to document the event. Many people spend long hours researching their own family history and all the same tools are available to research other people's stories as well.

JESSICA'S STORY

I received this story from a client who found undeniable historical evidence that confirmed the vivid past-life memories she had been experiencing.

I had a relatively normal, happy childhood in most regards. I was raised by a single mother; my parents separated when I was very young, so I never knew them together and their separation never affected me negatively.

I was always very skittish and afraid, especially at night. I slept with my mother in her bed until I was thirteen years old because I was afraid of the noises I heard in the house. I have memories of being five years old and having conversations with two men outside my bedroom window, apparitions. I could feel when I wasn't alone as a child, but I always thought of them as my friends, not knowing the difference.

My mother never specifically told me that she was psychic until I was much older, or that, therefore, I might be; I didn't understand what it was or how it worked. She just allowed me to be myself rather than impose herself.

One morning, when I was about nine years old, I awoke at about nine o'clock and told my mother that I had a great invention: Someone should create a blimp on which you can travel and eat. She looked at me and said, "There used to be one of those." I told her it probably worked better than the one I envisioned, because mine exploded.

My mom started to ask me about my dream, without alluding to anything historically. She asked me what it was about (she had an inkling at this point about what I had envisioned), and I told her that I had been a woman in my late fifties, maybe sixty years old, and I was traveling on a huge blimp. I was from another country. I can remember clearly what I was wearing as I gave them my ticket: a hat with a large, round brim and a large, heavy, ankle-length coat.

To my right there was a large stack of my luggage—I don't know why I had such a strong recollection of my luggage, but

I knew it was my luggage. I knew the person standing to my right was my current brother John (in this life), but he wasn't my brother in my dream. He was young and in his twenties. I knew that I was traveling alone and that I wasn't married.

The next thing I vividly recall was dinner in a dining room. The table area was sunken in the middle, with two bars that encircled the depressed dining room area. During the meal we flew over a field, and I can remember looking out the window and seeing grass and trees in the distance. The blimp's windows opened into the room instead of out, which I always thought was strange, and they didn't have screens on them.

It was fine dining; the china was white with blue writing—the image is still so clear in my head—and the next thing I knew, the dining room shifted and everything started falling to my left. Things were falling out of windows, and I remember holding on to the railing as long as I could and then falling against the wall. I felt the blimp hit the ground, but I knew in my dream that I didn't die.

After relaying all of this to my mom, she said to me, "Jessica, there was a blimp that blew up and it was called the *Hindenburg*." She didn't really say much more about it at the time.

A year later I went to visit my sister, who was living in Washington, DC, at the time. We went to the Smithsonian, where there was an exhibit about the *Hindenburg*, and we watched a documentary. All of my visions were validated as real and historical. The china, everything that happened, the way the blimp shifted, that there were survivors. On that particular day, bad weather had rolled into the New York area, forcing the blimp to reroute over a field in New Jersey, just as I had seen.

It wasn't until recently that I even thought to look up the passenger list and found one woman, traveling alone. The Smithsonian archives had a picture of her in a large hat, and there were specific stories about her having issues with her luggage, about her befriending a young twenty-four-year-old photographer, and about her dining alone and looking out a window as the *Hindenburg* came over the field and exploded. Her hands were burned by the fire. She wore a long, floor-length coat that saved her life. According to the information in the archives she was fifty-eight years old and named Margaret Mather. She was the only woman traveling without a husband, and she had come from visiting her family in London and flew out of Frankfurt, but was originally an American living in Rome.

This was the first of many visions I would have that would later be validated in some way months later. It was also the first time in my life that I realized we must live more than just one lifetime, and I really started talking with my mother about her abilities.

She always instructed me to protect myself and hold my boundaries against any negative force or energy. She also taught me that Ouija boards are dangerous and never to open a metaphysical door to let just anyone in, which is what a Ouija board allowed. She didn't really push anything else on me unless I specifically asked, other than a strong spiritual grounding.

But no encounter was more real or chilling than one I had in Italy. My family rented a centuries-old farmhouse in Tuscany, which happened to be haunted. One night I was awakened to feel my metal bed frame shaking on the terra-cotta floor as if it were being lifted and slammed back down. I ran into my mom's room; she could see who was there. It was a farmer who had passed away, sitting in a rocking chair. He didn't mean any harm, but he was definitely trying to startle me.

Next thing I knew, my mom's makeup bag went flying across the room from the nightstand. I threw the covers over my head in an attempt to surround myself with the white light of protection, as my mother had always taught me, but I could feel the fear getting the better of me. Later, I had finally managed to fall asleep when I heard a deep, heavy breathing in my right ear. My mom said, "Jessica, don't move." It was a deceased Roman soldier who had flung the makeup bag across the room and who was breathing in my ear.

That's when I learned the importance of strength and protecting yourself, and how fear can fuel the negative energy around you. Ever since then, I make sure that I always have a strong frame of mind when I'm in an uncomfortable situation. I haven't had an encounter since.

CHECK YOUR OWN AGENDA

As I've said, psychic abilities are a gift, and not all children are going to be psychic prodigies any more than every child is a piano or any other kind of prodigy. I know that every parent believes his or her child is special, and I believe that all children truly are special— but that doesn't mean they are all specially psychic. Some kids (and adults) are very psychic, some receive psychic information every once in a while, and some are about as psychic as a rock. In fact, you'd have to hit them in the head with a rock to get them to pay attention to what's coming at them from the spirit world.

In recent years, however, I've encountered many parents who are so eager to have a "special" child that they are quick to attribute his every hunch or statement about the future to having a heightened psychic sensibility. As I've said, all children are special in their own way, but if your kid says, "I think it's going to rain soon," and it does, that doesn't mean he's psychic. It could mean that he's just looked up and seen thunderclouds in the sky.

And if your three-year-old tells you there's a ghost under his bed, he might just have seen a scary movie or a television program about something psychic. Many parents tell me that they don't allow their children to watch scary movies or TV shows, but they forget that even some cartoon series, such as *Casper the Friendly Ghost* or *Scooby-Doo*, feature scary ghosts! Young children often have overactive imaginations, and even if a child is very specific about what the ghost looks like, he could well be calling upon his vivid imagination rather than his psychic abilities.

I often tell parents that if their child is reporting seeing "things that go bump in the night," and if they aren't sure what's *really* going on, they can put a hidden nanny cam in the child's room and see for themselves what's happening. If your child reports being awakened by spirits, and the video shows that he slept like a brick through the night, that will provide you with useful information. How you then choose to approach the child with what you've learned is truly up to you and will depend on your parenting style and what you know about your own child.

Imagination is a big part of any child's life, but in my experience (and I know that some child-development experts would disagree with me about this) it seems that about the time children reach puberty a switch flips and they become better able to distinguish what is real from what is not. If your child is old enough and mature enough to separate what is real from what is imagined, and if he comes to you and confides that he's been having psychic experiences, you need to take him seriously. But you also need to consider seriously that there could be other explanations for what he's experiencing—or thinks he's experiencing.

You need to assess what you're being told. Is it happening so consistently and so frequently that the chances of its being a mere coincidence are slim to none? Is your child generally given to flights of fancy, or is she in most respects a down-to-earth kid who tells it like it is? You know your own child, and you need to apply what you know to evaluating the validity of the experiences she's reporting.

And you also need to take a good look at what may be driving you to the conclusion that your child does, in fact, have heightened psychic abilities. Are there other explanations? Are you fascinated by the paranormal? Have you been doing a lot of reading about paranormal events? Have you been watching television programs that deal with the paranormal? If so, you may have internalized what you've been seeing or reading and, without even realizing it, attributed those abilities to your child.

One of the first things I do when I visit the home of a potentially psychic child is to look at what's on the bookshelves. If they're filled with books by psychic "stars," science fiction novels, or tapes of every paranormal series on television, I have to wonder whether the parents are primed to be "seeing" heightened abilities in their child that don't, in fact, exist.

BE OPEN BUT DON'T BE GULLIBLE

I like to tell people that there's a difference between being open to the paranormal and being gullible or even delusional. Every butterfly you see is not a sign from your deceased mother; it may just be the season when butterflies migrate. Personally, I prayed for nine years to receive an irrefutable sign from my own mother that her immortal soul was alive and well in the spirit world. I'd received little signs from time to time, but what I wanted was a full-blown apparition of her standing right in front of me. Then, one lovely late spring afternoon while I was mowing grass on my lawn tractor, I rounded a corner and there she stood. What was my first reaction? That I must have been having a stroke! Despite the fact that I communicate with the dead on a daily basis, I couldn't believe that I was actually seeing the spirit of my mother. After a second or two I realized that I definitely hadn't suffered a stroke, nor was I suffering from heat exhaustion, and, therefore, what I was seeing must be real. There was no rational way to explain or deny it. My prayers had been answered. For three to five precious seconds, I was reunited with my mother. Sadly, not every sign from the afterlife is that clear and undeniable.

Generally speaking, I've found that if a child is acting "normal" in every other aspect of her life, if she isn't given to creating unnecessary drama or exaggeration, then what she's saying about her psychic experiences is probably true. But, as a parent, it's still your responsibility to investigate what she reports to the best of your ability and rule out other explanations without ruling out the psychic truth.

WHATEVER YOU DO, DON'T PANIC

If you've carefully assessed alternative explanations and determined that you truly believe your child is psychic, there's no need to panic.

A woman came up to me at one of my events and told me that her four-year-old son was being harassed by a spirit in her home. She was clearly terrified and told me that she constantly prayed with her child for the spirit to leave and was repeatedly sprinkling her house with holy water. What I tried to explain to her (and she was clearly not buying) is that her child, as a four-year-old, did not have the ability to fully understand what he was experiencing and that her reaction as his mother was making him more fearful than he would otherwise have been.

Every child is born with only two fears: the fear of falling (or being dropped) and the fear of loud noises. All other fears are learned. So if a child expresses fear of ghosts or demons or monsters or the bogeyman, he has somehow learned about those beings and also learned to fear them.

Any child who is having experiences he doesn't understand or can't explain needs his parents to reassure and protect him. For example, Nick (we'll be hearing more about Nick in chapter 4) and Anissa, two children who appeared together on a season 3 episode of *Psychic Kids*, were terrified of sleeping in their own rooms because ghosts would often visit them during the night. Nick was so traumatized by the nightly visits, some of which included physical assaults, that he began having frequent night terrors.

Children who have night terrors are usually described as bolting upright with their eyes wide open, a look of fear and panic on their faces, sweating, breathing fast, having heart palpitations, sometimes even screaming. They may be confused, inconsolable, even unable to recognize people who should be familiar to them.

When Anissa and Nick arrived to begin filming their episode, I discovered that neither of them would take a shower or even go to the bathroom unless a parent was standing just outside the partly open door. Their paranormal experiences had left them suffering from what could only be described as post-traumatic stress disorder, a serious psychological condition that is a lasting consequence of traumatic ordeals causing intense fear, helplessness, or horror.

DR. KARA LARSON TALKS ABOUT ANISSA

I have been a practicing pediatrician for the past twelve years. I have had a lot of parents approach me with concerns about their children's fears and anxieties. So when my coworker and very good friend Kim told me that her daughter, Anissa, was having problems sleeping in her own bed at night, I didn't think twice, even when she added that Anissa was afraid because she was seeing spirits. This is a fairly common claim among young children. But when I heard that Anissa was also seeing spirits during the day at school, at soccer practice, at the mall, etc., and that she was able to talk and communicate with them, I took notice.

As a physician, I had a lot of concern for Anissa and a lot of doubt about her claims. Was she really able to see and communicate with ghosts and spirits, or was she just a very anxious child with an overactive imagination? Worse yet, was Anissa suffering from hallucinations or delusions and seriously mentally ill? One of the basic principles of science is to rely on evidence and proof whenever possible. This is the most desirable way to practice medicine. "How do you get proof that a child is seeing and talking to ghosts?" I thought. Not so easy to accomplish.

As Kim began to tell me about all of the things Anissa could see and do, my doubt and disbelief changed to awe and amazement. Kim gave me countless examples of Anissa's looking at a photograph of someone who had passed on, talking with him, and then giving very specific details about that person's life, illness, and death. She told me about Anissa's telling a schoolmate's mother she had seen a small dog running around in the yard with a toy in its mouth, only to find out later that the family's dog had died twelve years before and that it had loved to run around the yard chasing the kids . . . with a ball in its mouth. She told me about the spirit of Anissa's great-grandfather, who had appeared to her in a baseball uniform, and that she then was able to pick him out of an old photograph of a baseball team. This was despite the fact that he had died when Kim was only ten and Anissa had never seen pictures of him before.

"This is real," I told Kim. "Children who are hallucinating or having delusions will see and hear things, but not things that can be independently verified. I think she really is seeing and hearing this stuff!" As a skeptic, this was proof enough for me. My eyes were opened to an entirely new perspective on the world. I became a believer.

Before meeting Anissa, a gap existed in my thinking as a pediatrician. Prior to hearing her story, no explanation for her claims other than internal strife or mental illness would have crossed my mind. Unfortunately, many in my profession have that same confined view.

An oath that all physicians take to become a physician is "First, do no harm." I recently visited with another child who was placed in an inpatient psychiatric unit and medicated in an attempt to "treat" his condition. He and his family were deeply harmed by that traumatic experience. He is not alone.

Certainly, there are children who truly suffer from mental illness. But there also are children who have psychic abilities. The responsibility in part lies with medical and mental health care providers to help distinguish between the two. Treating a psychic kid as if he were mentally ill is just as damaging as not treating one who is mentally ill.

Psychic children are special, just as all children are special. Psychic children have gifts and abilities, just as all children have gifts and abilities. Male or female, black or white, gay or straight, psychic or not, all children are precious and valuable. But they are still children.

These children, like all children, need love and support and validation. They need love and support and validation from their parents, family members, and friends, and also from their teachers and therapists and health care professionals. They need love and support and validation from all of society. To ignore or condemn or bully or shame or even discount or dismiss these children is harmful to them and harmful to all of us. Anissa is fortunate. She receives love and support and validation for her abilities. More kids should be so lucky.

One of our goals on the program was to empower both Anissa and Nick so that they would feel safe and comfortable being alone at appropriate times. To get them accustomed to sleeping alone in a room, we took a few baby steps and allowed them to sleep in a room together one night. We instructed their parents how to move forward once they had returned home, with the goal of helping the children to reclaim their bedrooms as their personal space. Among the suggestions we gave them, which you can use with your own child if he or she is afraid of sleeping alone, are the following:

- Without traumatizing the child, firmly but lovingly make it known that the goal is to facilitate his feeling safe and comfortable sleeping in his own room.

- Encourage him to talk about his fears. Talking about fears often helps children feel better. Many times children are unable to pinpoint exactly what they're afraid of until they start discussing it. Talking about fears also helps parents get an idea of exactly what their children are afraid of and how serious the fear is. This information is useful when coming up with ways to help children confront their fears. Parents should also try to use these discussion times to let their children know that all people experience fear at one time or another and that it's okay to be afraid when fears are justifiable.

- Spend a few minutes with the child in his bedroom as he is settling into bed for the night. Reassure the child that you are close by and available if truly needed.

- Teach the child the empowerment skills discussed in this book. Fully support him in facing his fears.

- Teach him how to use positive self-talk. Positive self-talk is saying positive things about oneself to oneself. It is a very powerful tool for children to have. The more children repeat good things to themselves about themselves, the more likely they will be to believe them and incorporate those positive feelings that go along with them. For example, a child who is afraid of the dark can be taught to say things like, "I'm not afraid. It's just dark. Mommy and Daddy are in the next room. There's nothing in here that can hurt me."

- Allow the child to sleep with a night-light or connect a dimmer switch to his bedroom light so that the light can be adjusted to a level that provides comfort to the child. Some children also feel safe if they have a flashlight they can turn on whenever they become anxious about the darkness.

- For younger children, it is often possible to fill a spray bottle with plain tap water, tell them that the "magic potion" in the bottle is called "Go Away, Monster" or "Ghost Be Gone," and instruct them to spray the ghost, goblin, or monster to make it disappear.

- Realize that the child may not initially sleep in his own room for an entire night. He may become fearful and sneak into bed with a parent or sibling. Even if he stays in his room for part of the night, congratulate him on his progress and continue the process of acclimating him to sleeping through the night in his own bedroom. Taking baby steps will often lead to the desired results. You may even want to make a chart in order to provide a visual record of the child's progress.

- *Never* criticize, make fun of, or punish a child for being fearful.

Happily, Anissa and Nick are now able to bathe, go to the bathroom, and sleep alone without fear of being harmed.

IN HER OWN WORDS: WHERE ANISSA IS NOW

Being on the show made me stronger and more open to my abilities. I no longer feel "trapped inside my box." I have become more intuitive and I do not feel so alone. I've met so many amazing people because of the show. My life is certainly better. Chip and Edy helped me to face my fears and made me stronger and more confident. I will always remember—as Chip always told me—to have "no fear, no doubt" in my life.

Since I appeared on the show, I have been able to speak more freely about my abilities because I know that I am no longer alone. I've met a few other psychic kids and I have even been able to help some of them, which makes me very happy. I've done some investigations with paranormal groups. Without the show, I don't know where I would be. Most likely, still scared and feeling alone. I love my life even more since being on *Psychic Kids* and I am so happy to have the support of my family, friends, and now my *Psychic Kids* family. I've learned a lot and I want to continue helping others the way my family and I received help from the show.

And her mother adds:

"Yes, the experience changed my life, the life of my daughter, and the lives of our family and friends who love and support Anissa. Anissa was this beautiful child who lived in fear of what she did not understand. Her fear would often affect her younger brother, Jacob, as well. He didn't understand anything about what Anissa was afraid of and it greatly affected our family dynamic. We kept a lot of what was going on with Anissa to ourselves, which really isn't our style. We are a pretty open family, sharing our thoughts and feelings with others, but this was just not the case when it came to what we were experiencing within our own home with Anissa. When we were running out of resources and not knowing where to turn, the *Psychic*

Kids show seemed like a great possibility for getting help. When Anissa's story was chosen to be part of the show, we had no idea how life-changing it would be. It is the best thing we have done thus far when it comes to helping Anissa understand and accept her abilities. Since the show, I have seen Anissa thrive with a sense of awareness and confidence. I think the biggest thing the show has given to me, as a mother of a psychic child, is the sense of empowerment. I am no longer afraid! As a mom, all you want to do is love your children, to be a good teacher and role model, but I could not teach Anissa when it came to her psychic abilities. We have been given tools that help Anissa to be in control of her own sense of self and the world around her. I've learned that I need to let go of the fear and worry and accept the fact that Anissa will be *my* teacher. *Our* teacher! And when I put all of this together, I feel empowered and free."

In another, not-so-dissimilar case, Olivia S. (not to be confused with Olivia K.) was a twelve-year-old living in an old Victorian-style house in New England and was being visited during the night by three different male entities and one old woman who were scaring the life out of her—to the point where she would no longer sleep in her own room or even stay at home by herself. It turned out that the house had previously served as a nursing home and hospice facility and that these were the spirits of patients who had died there. Sometimes spirits do get "stuck" and remain in the place where they died rather than moving on to the spiritual realm. They're not generally malevolent, just confused, but they can, nevertheless, be terrifying for a child who doesn't understand what's happening, which was exactly Olivia S.'s situation.

During the filming of the *Psychic Kids* episode that featured Olivia S. and her family, I asked my dear friend Charlotte Scott, the energy worker whom we met earlier in this chapter, to consult on the case. Together, Charlotte and I helped Olivia S. to accept the fact that, since none of these spirits had ever exhibited any animosity toward her, she could safely anticipate that they would not hurt her in the future. With this understanding, she was able to change her perception of what was happening and overcome her fear of the spirits in her home. And to help her step into her power, Charlotte and I (along with Amy, the other psychic kid who appeared in the episode) helped Olivia S. to perform various banishment rituals, such as smudging (see page 114), designed to clear her home of any negative energies or entities that might have invaded the space.

IN HER OWN WORDS: WHERE OLIVIA S. IS NOW

The experience of being on *Psychic Kids* changed my life, because I had never met others who had the same abilities as me. Before I was on the show, I was terrified of what I could do and what I could see. Chip really helped me by calming me down and telling me to listen to what the spirits are trying to say to me, because every spirit wants to be heard and some need to know that they should cross over to the light in order to be happy again. It's been really helpful and fun to learn about these things. In the future, I will use what I have learned to help other people, not just myself. No fear! No doubt!

My life has been good since the show. It was the best time of my life because of Chip Coffey and Edy Nathan. If I hadn't gotten their help, I wouldn't be happy because I didn't know what was going on with me. I was seeing all these spirits and I thought I was crazy. But now I know I'm not! I have met psychic kids from other episodes of the show and we keep in contact with each other. I listen to what they know and tell them what's going on at my house and around me. They help me to understand things I haven't learned yet. I'm not alone in this world. There are other kids just like me!

And her mother adds:

"The show could not have come at a better time. The fear that was consuming Olivia had affected every part of our day-to-day life. We had exhausted all of our resources trying to figure out what she was seeing and experiencing. It prevented her from enjoying the safe and happy life that every twelve-year-old should have. As soon as we met Chip and his team, I knew inside that our search for answers about what had been going on for the past five and a half years was coming to an end. It was one of the most emotional and inspiring experiences of my life, watching my daughter emerge out of fear and move into a better understanding of who she is.

"Life has never been better! After almost six years, Olivia now sleeps in her own bedroom and stays in the house by herself (which she would never do before), and whenever she sees spirits outside the home, she takes notes if they speak to her or draws them when they remain silent. She embraces their presence instead of running away in fear. She has remained in contact with Chip and several of the other youngsters from previous episodes. They have taught her skills on how to recognize what she senses empathically. Instead of absorbing all of the energy, she has begun to know which feelings are hers and which feelings belong to others. Most importantly, she has learned how to protect herself from negative energy. I am more grateful than I could ever say in words. I feel that being a part of *Psychic Kids* saved my daughter's life."

As a parent, if your child sees that what he's encountering or what he tells you he's encountering is causing you to panic, he will only feel that he can't count on you to keep him safe, and that will just make him even more afraid. However you approach and react to the paranormal, your child will learn from that and mirror your response. And if you start to treat him like a freak, or like someone in need of an exorcism, he'll start to feel like a freak. Or, even worse, he'll stop confiding in you.

Happily, I'm finding that more and more people are, at the very least, beginning to entertain the possibility that people—kids included—are able to receive paranormal information. And I believe that the more open we are, the more we evolve and the more psychic we become. Your child may be ahead of the curve, but he's not a freak, and he certainly won't be helped by your treating him like one.

The basics of parenting a psychic kid are really not so very different from those of raising any other child. Being psychic is certainly a major part of who your child is, but it is not the only—and maybe not the most important—part. Maybe he's a piano prodigy or she's a precocious painter; maybe your kid is a computer whiz or a natural at learning languages. Those are certainly important parts of anyone's identity that need to be nurtured and encouraged. The goal of parents should be to support and empower their child, and that goal, of course, applies just as much—if not even more—to the parents of psychic kids.

CHECKLIST FOR PARENTS

- Reassure and support your specially gifted psychic kids.

- Seek appropriate medical and/or psychiatric help to be certain there is no underlying physical or emotional problem.

- If your child is generally truthful, assume that he is also being truthful about his psychic experiences.

- Do your own homework to validate what your child is telling you.

- Don't let anyone misdiagnose or medicate your child for a mental illness he doesn't have.

- Don't let your desire to have a "special" child lead you to "see" abilities that aren't there—wishing doesn't make it so.

- Don't thrust your own fears of the paranormal upon your child.

CHAPTER THREE

Controlling and Managing Psychic Gifts

One of my own personal mantras is "No fear, no doubt," and I share it with others, including almost every psychic kid I work with. These children and their families are often filled with both fear and doubt, so helping them to address those issues is very important.

Fear and doubt are two of the biggest obstacles we face. They can immobilize us and prevent us from becoming who and what we are supposed to be. Call me foolish, naïve, or just plain stupid, but I do not allow fear to overpower me. And neither should any psychic kid. That's not to say that I suggest taking foolish risks or making reckless decisions, because I don't. But I do believe that I am divinely protected, and I cling to that belief whenever I am at risk of losing my inner strength and courage. Psychic kids need to find ways to feel safe and protected, and their parents are generally the ones who can help them to do that.

FEAR OF BEING "WRONG"

It is not uncommon for anyone who receives psychic information to question its validity. Uncertainty and distrust are very common among psychic kids, primarily because they are confused about how or why they are receiving psychic information in the first place.

I remember, as a young boy, visiting my godparents on Long Island and being pulled aside by a gaggle of Italian ladies of every age, shape, and size who wanted me to give them readings. I also remember being somewhat nervous because I didn't want the information I was giving them to be wrong. I always felt a great sense of relief when the ladies told me that the predictions I had made had come to pass. They never paid me for my services, but I was always rewarded with delicious Italian food!

Then, when I began working as a professional psychic and medium, I continued to worry about being right and providing correct information to my clients. How could I be sure that the information I was intuitively receiving was accurate? Sometimes, if I couldn't decipher the meaning of a message I was receiving, I would censor myself and not pass that message along to my client. And then I learned a valuable lesson.

I was doing a reading for a woman named Tara, who was distraught because her family had recently moved to a new home and she no longer felt her deceased father's spirit around her. "I used to feel him quite often in our old home, but since we moved, I haven't felt him at all. Doesn't my father know where to find me?" she asked.

I told her I surely didn't believe she had "lost" her dad and suggested that he was probably just "doing his own thing" in the spirit world and not overly concerned about what was happening in the living world. Suddenly, as I was telling her these things, a single word entered my mind: waterfall. "What does this mean?" I wondered. Did the family visit Niagara Falls, Victoria Falls, Iguazu Falls? Since I didn't understand the meaning of the word, I censored myself and continued with Tara's reading.

I did deliver many meaningful and comforting messages from her father, but, at the end of the reading, I decided to just bite the bullet. So I said to Tara, "Earlier, your father said a single word that didn't make any sense to me, but perhaps it will mean something to you. The word that I heard was 'waterfall.'" Tara gasped and began to sob. "Now I'm sure my dad knows where we moved because there is a lovely waterfall in the backyard of our new home," she said.

From that day forward, I have delivered every bit of information I receive during readings, whether I understand the message or not. With Tara, I almost censored the most meaningful message I could have provided, and I certainly do not want to make that mistake with any client ever again.

Sometimes, clients don't understand the significance of certain information that is provided to them during a reading. They can be caught up in the moment and feeling anxious or emotional, so they may not be fully "connecting the dots." I always tell my clients to hang on to any information that doesn't seem to make sense, to think about it after the reading, and generally, they will be able to decipher the message.

I also advise clients, if they feel comfortable doing so, to talk with family members or friends about anything they don't understand. Very often, someone else will be able to help them figure it out or will have information they didn't have at the time of the reading. Here is a perfect example of how this sometimes occurs, as told by my client services manager, Rebecca:

REBECCA MEETS UNCLE RALPH

"I am a desperate woman," I told my good friend Blair over a glass of wine. "I've lost my grandmother's heirloom sapphire ring and I can't find it anywhere. It's driving me crazy, not knowing whether I've just misplaced it or it's truly lost. I've been looking for it for over a year and I'm starting to lose all hope that it will ever be found. I think I need to find a reliable psychic."

Blair, who worked at that time as a nurse at an Atlanta-area hospital, has always had an interest in anything spiritual or paranormal. She told me that if we could find a good and reputable psychic, we'd go together and get readings.

About a month later I received a phone call from Blair. "I think I've found our psychic," she said excitedly. "A few days ago, this guy came in for some outpatient surgery and it turns out that he's a psychic. Before he went into surgery, he told one of the other nurses some things about her life that were totally accurate. And then, while he was in the recovery room, right after surgery, he grabbed another nurse by the arm and said, 'I have something I need to tell you.' That nurse was completely blown away by what this guy said. His name is Chip Coffey. Why don't you see if you can find him on the Internet and make appointments for both of us?"

I found Chip's website and called him to make appointments for Blair and me. These days, Chip does all of his private readings for clients by telephone, but back then, he did some readings in person, so a few weeks later, Blair and I met Chip at his office just north of Atlanta.

When it came time for my reading, I told Chip that I had come to see him hoping to find a ring I had lost. "It matches this bracelet I am wearing," I told him. Chip reached out and touched the bracelet and immediately said, "This belonged to your paternal grandmother and her name begins with a C, but it sounds like a K." He was eerily accurate! The ring and bracelet had been given to me by my father's mother, whose name was Catarina, but everyone called her Kay.

I started to tear up and Chip looked to the side as if someone was talking to him over his shoulder. "Don't cry," he said. "Your grandmother is telling me that the ring isn't gone for good."

Chip proceeded to tell me that my grandmother had circulatory problems with her feet and legs, and before I could answer, he quickly asked, "Was she a double amputee?" By that time, I was in complete shock, with tears streaming down my cheeks, as I nodded yes. Before she died, it had been necessary to amputate both of Grandma Kay's legs. He looked again to his side and what he said next is something I will never forget: "She's telling me to tell you not to think of her that way anymore because that is not the way she is now."

Chip took a deep breath and said, "Okay, let's see if she can tell us where the ring is." He said that Grandma Kay told him it was in a jewelry box with a blue velvet lining. I had repeatedly searched for the ring in my jewelry box, but it has a red lining. "It's near a place where the carpet on the floor is pulled away from the wall or there's a rug that won't stay in place," he continued.

What Chip was describing made no sense to me, and I was somewhat disappointed. After being so right about Grandma Kay, how could he be going so far off track about the location of her ring?

A strange look came over Chip's face. "Hold on," he said. "Someone else, another spirit, is trying to come through to us." He told me that this rarely happens during his readings, but when it does, he knows the interrupting spirit has something very important to share.

He told me that the spirit's name was Ralph and he was some-how related to my father. I replied that there was no one named Ralph in my father's family. Undaunted, Chip said that Ralph was telling him about a house fire and something about under-ground water or wells. "He's also telling me a pretty gross story about spitting tobacco juice in someone's hand," Chip told me.

By this time, I'd stopped taking notes. My reading had started off so accurately and now it appeared to have taken a few very wrong turns. Chip sensed my frustration and confusion. He smiled at me—a knowing smile—and said, "Ralph says to ask your father."

Several days later, I phoned my dad to ask him about Ralph, the spirit who had dropped by during my reading. I told him what Chip had said during my reading and he was silent for a few moments. Then he said, "Rebecca, there *was* a man named Ralph in my family. My uncle Ralph. He was my grandfather's brother and my favorite uncle when I was growing up."

I was surprised that I'd never heard of Uncle Ralph and even more surprised by what my dad said next. "Uncle Ralph's house burned down when I was just a boy. And he taught us kids how to dowse for underground water by using a willow reed," Dad said.

"But what about the disgusting story about spitting tobacco juice in someone's hand?" I asked. My dad laughed heartily and said, "Uncle Ralph was quite a character. He chewed tobacco and sometimes, as a sick joke, he would tell us kids to hold out our hands, close our eyes, and he'd give us a present. When we did so, he'd spit tobacco juice in our outstretched palms."

I was in complete shock! Chip had hit a bull's-eye with his information about Uncle Ralph. But he had totally missed the mark about where to find my grandma Kay's missing ring. Hadn't he?

I told my dad what his mother had said about the location of her ring and he again grew silent. "Rebecca, that sounds a lot like your mom's built-in jewelry box in her walk-in closet here at our house," he said.

"That's impossible," I retorted. "Why would the ring be in Mom's jewelry box? And besides, there is no carpet in her closet. The floor is hardwood." What I didn't know was that my mom had recently purchased a scatter rug for the floor of her closet. Dad informed me that they called it "the traveling rug" because it never stayed in place and they'd been meaning to buy some double-stick tape to secure it to the floor.

"I'm going right now to look in your mom's jewelry box to see if the ring is there," my dad said. "I'll call you back in a few minutes."

My mind raced as I waited for his call. There was no logical way my ring would turn up in my mother's jewelry box, but logic flew out the window when I spoke to my dad a few minutes later. He informed me that he had found the ring in Mom's jewelry box with a blue lining, just a step or two away from the rug that wouldn't stay in place. It was precisely as Chip had described!

I phoned Chip a few days later to tell him I'd found the ring and validated the information about Ralph, and I apologized for doubting him. He laughed and told me that he was happy for me. We stayed in touch periodically over the next few months, and within a year he hired me to book his clients for private readings.

When I think back on my first meeting with Chip, I realize that I would have never discussed the reading with my dad unless Uncle Ralph had come through. Hearing the stories Chip had told me about his long-dead uncle had gotten my dad's attention, which led to us talking about—and then finding—the lost ring. Thanks, Uncle Ralph!

Now I tell all Chip's clients to take good notes during their readings and never simply dismiss or discount any information he provides, because it's very likely that soon they will discover that Chip was right. Just as I did!

One last thing I always tell my clients, with regard to information they may not initially understand during a reading, is never to stretch anything too far just to make it fit. If the suspected meaning of a message isn't pretty darned obvious and clear, then that isn't the correct meaning of the message.

WHAT KIDS NEED TO KNOW ABOUT PSYCHIC ACCURACY

With time and experience I've come to understand that some of the messages I receive will not be immediately meaningful to my clients and that it serves no useful purpose for me to constantly doubt the validity of the messages. My duty—and that of every psychic—is simply to deliver the information I get from those in spirit. But I've also come to understand that psychics don't know everything and no psychic is ever right every time. Even the "best" psychics have an estimated accuracy rate of around 70 to 80 percent. Therefore, anyone who seeks counsel from a psychic should use good common sense and discretion when deciding how to use the information he or she provides.

Those who get readings from psychics should know that there is no guarantee of accuracy, but not everyone does. Therefore, many professional psychics, especially those with Internet websites, post legal disclaimers. On my own website, I have posted the following:

- Please be advised that no psychic reading can predict, forecast, diagnose or provide information with absolute certainty.

- No guarantees or assurances of any kind are given and Chip Coffey will not be held accountable for any interpretations or decisions made by recipients based on information provided during readings.

- For entertainment purposes only.

- For medical concerns, please consult with a physician.

- For legal matters, please contact an attorney or law enforcement.

Skeptics and critics use such disclaimers as proof that all psychics are charlatans. Hogwash! There are very few absolutes in life. In reality, consulting a psychic is really not so different from trusting your stock-broker to invest your money in companies he believes will earn a good return on your investment and then blaming him when the stocks do not perform well. Both psychics and stockbrokers do their best to provide quality services, but, unfortunately, there is no guarantee of the outcome.

Those same skeptics and critics frequently focus on the statement "For entertainment purposes only" that appears on many psychics' websites. I cringed at being told to post that statement on my site, but my attorney suggested using this verbiage would help to dissuade people from filing frivolous lawsuits.

Therefore, it is important that all psychic kids understand that they are not omniscient and that no one should expect them to be so. Once they accept their very human fallibility they will be better able to banish both the fear of being wrong and any doubt they might have about the messages they are receiving.

HELP YOUR KID TO COPE

Olivia K., the young girl we met in chapter 2, is now a confident young woman with a very bright future who is ready to take on any challenge that comes her way. But when she first arrived to participate in our three-day retreat, she told us that if she didn't get help deal-ing with her psychic experiences she thought she would "go insane." That's a powerful and frightening statement for any teenager to make, and I knew that she was desperate for some way to take control of her own life. What happened during the seventy-two hours she spent with us is that her perceptions and feelings were validated, and she discovered that she could call on her power at will, rather than have the psychic information come at her more or less randomly whether she wanted it or not. As a result, for the first time Olivia felt that she was in charge of her abilities—the captain of her own ship, if you will. And because of that, she began to feel proud of her gift rather than victimized by it.

A gift is only a gift if it is perceived as such. Therefore, it's important for psychic kids to feel safe enough to discuss what they're experiencing and get the help they need to harness and manage their abilities.

On *Psychic Kids*, when we take our young psychics and their parents on a three-day "retreat" to a location that is known to be haunted, we give them the opportunity to express and explore their abilities in an atmosphere where they will be safe and supported. In that environment we are able to work with them and show them how to own what they know. The vast majority of psychic kids I've met are extremely bright and, when they're allowed to speak without fear of ridicule or unwelcome repercussions, extremely articulate about what's going on in their lives.

Based on the feedback we've received from viewers, it appears that many parents have used the program as a kind of tool that provides them with an opening for discussion with their own kids. Now I have the opportunity to expand upon what we have been able to convey within the constraints of a one-hour broadcast (and without any commercial interruptions).

ARE YOU PSYCHIC, TOO?

One way parents can create safety and a sense of normalcy is to share their own experiences with their child. I have found that psychic abilities often run in families, as they do in mine. Because I always knew they would be open and receptive, I never hesitated to share my interest and experiences with my parents, and I was always comfortable taking ownership of who and what I am. I believe that if a psychic child knows he's inherited his gift—in the same way he's inherited his blond hair or blue eyes—it will help him to feel more "normal." (Of course, he may also wonder why he couldn't have inherited someone's computer skills or prowess on the basketball court instead, but you can't please everybody all the time!)

One mother named Karen, who contacted me after watching *Psychic Kids*, confided that psychic abilities seemed to be handed down by the women of her family and that she, too, had had psychic experiences as a child but had blocked them out. Apparently she'd hoped that if she didn't acknowledge what was happening it would just go away. And now, she said, she'd been doing the same thing in response to what her daughter, Linda, was telling her about her own psychic experiences. Because Karen had always looked upon her gift as a burden, she'd been trying to deny—rather than validate—Linda's experiences. But, having watched *Psychic Kids* and having seen how supportive it could be for a child to know that her parent shared her gift, Karen had told Linda that she, too, was psychic. And once she realized how much confidence and pride that knowledge inspired in her child, she deeply regretted not having done it much sooner.

Strange and unexplainable things do happen in the world around us. And if a parent, other relative, or close friend lets a psychic kid know that he or she has also had psychic or paranormal experiences, it can help the child feel validated, less alone, and more "normal." (After all, if his mom or grandma or uncle Bill is psychic or has seen spirits and isn't weird, well then, neither is he.) And it can also help him to realize that his parent and others really do understand what he's experiencing and may have valuable guidance to share.

As I mentioned earlier, my mother also had psychic abilities, and so did her paternal grandmother. Some of my cousins have also shared their own personal psychic and paranormal experiences with me.

My cousin Frank, for example, was filled with grief when his mother, Betty Jo, died in 2005, and for years after, he found it difficult to let go of that grief. Late one night, Frank awoke to find his mother standing at the foot of his bed. Although she did not speak, Frank said that just seeing her made him feel joyful and comforted. Several days later, he told his sister, Kim, about their mother's nocturnal visit and was shocked to learn that Kim had also been visited by Betty Jo on the very same night.

My cousin Kenny, who has been sharing my home in Atlanta for several years, has also experienced spirit visitations. At the time he came to live with me I had a small dog named Bo, who was very precious to both of us. Sadly, a couple of years later, Bo contracted cancer and died. Several times since Bo's passing, Kenny has mentioned catching glimpses of Bo's spirit, both inside the house and in the backyard. Although Kenny was raised in a fairly fundamentalist Christian family, he is perfectly willing to accept that unexplainable things do happen in the world around us.

Finally, here's a strange experience I personally shared with several of my family members. My cousin Joye was scheduled to undergo a rather routine surgical procedure at a hospital in Atlanta. While she was in the operating room, as her mother, my aunt Helen, and I sat in the waiting room, my cell phone rang.

"What the hell are you guys trying to pull?" I heard when I answered the call. It was Suzanne, Joye's daughter, calling from South Carolina, and she sounded very upset. I had no idea what she was talking about and I told her so.

"You know very well what I'm talking about," she yelled at me. "I just got a call from my mother. She said that she had died on the operating table, that she was calling to say goodbye and she'd always love me. Then the phone went dead. I don't know what kind of sick joke y'all are trying to pull, but I don't think it's one bit funny!"

I tried to assure Suzanne that there was absolutely no way her mother could have called her because she was on the operating table, under anesthesia. But Suzanne remained unconvinced, insisting that she had most assuredly received the call.

Later that morning, when Joye's surgeon came to speak with her mother and me, he told us something that sent a cold shiver up my spine. During the operation, Joye had "crashed" and was clinically dead for several seconds! Thankfully, the surgical team was able to revive and stabilize her.

As impossible as it sounds, it appeared that Joye had somehow reached out, across time and miles, to her daughter, Suzanne, during those brief seconds when she was teetering between life and death.

HELPING KIDS UNDERSTAND DEATH AND DYING

An inescapable fact of life is that every living thing eventually dies. Therefore, it is inevitable that, at some point, a child will be exposed to death. He may find a dead bird while playing outside. Or his beloved pet may die. Or a relative may pass away.

Psychic kids, however, may also be exposed to death in a very different way: Many of them are visited by the dead, often making them feel scared and confused, not only about what they are experiencing but also about death itself. Many of them are frightened by seeing ghosts and spirits and wonder, "Why is this happening to me?" Although no one really knows the answer to that question, I believe that children who possess heightened paranormal abilities are often like magnets for ghosts and spirits. Somehow, those entities know that the child has the ability to sense them or see them, and for any number of possible reasons, they make their presence known. This will almost certainly be distressing for the child, and others in his life, until the child learns to accept them or—in the case of malevolent beings—banish them from his life.

Death and dying are topics most of us would prefer to avoid because we don't like to think about our own mortality or the loss of our loved ones. Many parents, therefore, find it difficult to discuss death with their children. But that difficult discussion becomes unavoidable when death hits close to home.

Just how much a child is able to comprehend about death depends greatly on age and maturity. Children under the age of two have little concept of death, yet will miss the deceased and react to the sadness of others who are feeling the loss. Two-to-four-year-olds find it difficult to comprehend that death is permanent and will often ask when the deceased is coming back. Five-to-ten-year-olds begin to understand the finality of death and often have many questions about it. Then, by the time children reach adolescence, they are able to understand both the concept and the permanence of death.

When a death occurs, children should be allowed to ask questions and parents need to answer them as fully and clearly as possible. Use language that is familiar and age-appropriate to the child, but be wary of using euphemisms, such as "Uncle John has gone to sleep," or "Grandma went to a better place," that could confuse them even more. Young children might then worry that when they go to sleep, they won't wake up, or that when someone goes away on vacation, he won't return.

Children may ask what happens after death, and how a parent responds will often depend on individual beliefs about the afterlife. Some believe in heaven and hell. Others believe in a spiritual realm or alternate dimension. Atheists believe that when you die, you're dead, end of story. In reality, however, no one actually knows what occurs after death. It is one of the greatest mysteries of life. I remember very clearly standing outside, looking up at the stars, just after my aunt Polly died and muttering aloud, "Well, Aunt Polly, now you know the secret." And that is precisely what death is: the ultimate secret, known only to those who have experienced it. Some people, however, may have gotten a glimpse of the afterlife.

Dr. Raymond Moody is the world's leading authority on near-death experiences (NDEs), a phrase he coined in the late 1970s to describe a phenomenon that is generally reported when an individual is very close to death or has been declared clinically dead. In his work as a medical doctor, author, and lecturer, Dr. Moody has encountered thousands of people claiming to have had this type of experience. His book *Life After Life* is widely accepted as the definitive book on the subject and has sold more than thirteen million copies worldwide.

From a study of a hundred and fifty people who had either clinically died or almost died, Dr. Moody concluded that there are nine common experiences associated with NDEs:

- hearing sounds, such as buzzing
- a feeling of peace and painlessness
- having an out-of-body experience
- a feeling of traveling through a tunnel
- a feeling of rising into the heavens
- seeing people, often dead relatives
- meeting a spiritual being, such as Jesus or God
- seeing a review of one's life
- feeling a sense of reluctance to return to life

Personally, I have encountered several children and numerous adults, including my own mother, who claim to have had an NDE. One of those children was a young boy from Canada named Kyle.

Twelve-year-old Kyle was riding his bike one summer day when he was hit by a car as he rounded a corner. He was thrown to the pavement, very badly hurt, and drifting in and out of consciousness. An ambulance arrived quickly to the scene of the accident and paramedics began working on Kyle.

Several minutes later, according to Kyle, "everything stopped for a moment and went blank." "And," he says, "in the next instant, I remember watching everything from off to the side and a little bit above. I felt sorry for the poor boy lying in the middle of the street and then I realized that the boy was me."

Kyle says he didn't feel any pain at all and, in fact, felt detached from his physical body, as if it didn't really belong to him anymore.

Suddenly, everything around him disappeared and Kyle was enveloped in a bright white fog. He felt like he was traveling very fast through a "tunnel" and heard a droning noise that sounded like a blend of "soft humming and the wind blowing." He says that the best way he can describe what he experienced is that it was somewhat like flying through dense clouds on an airplane.

"I could see shadowy figures in the distance, up ahead of me, and as I moved closer to them, I saw my grandmother step forward," Kyle remembers. "I was really confused, but I also felt so happy to see her because she had died about a year ago and I missed her a lot."

"Kylie, you really have to be more careful from now on when you're riding that bike," his grandma said to him, smiling and shaking her head. She wrapped her arms around Kyle, hugged him close, and that's when he felt a huge pain in his chest.

Kyle later learned that the pain he felt in his chest was caused by the defibrillator paramedics used to restart his heart. "The next thing I remember, I was lying on a gurney in the back of the ambulance," Kyle recalls.

The next day, he told his parents about the strange experience. "I told them how good and safe it felt when my grandma hugged me," he remembered. That's when his mom gasped and began to sob.

When she had somewhat regained her composure, Kyle's mother shared her own story. "When they let us see you in the emergency room, I leaned over to give you a kiss and I smelled my mother's perfume on you. I thought it was just my imagination, but now it makes sense."

Kyle and his family believe that he had a near-death experience and was briefly reunited with his grandmother. Today, he is a college student in his midtwenties and says that his life changed after his NDE.

"I wouldn't say that I became a psychic kid after the accident, but I did sometimes know things were going to happen before they actually did. And I often felt things about people or places around me," Kyle says. "And those things still happen every now and then."

Sharing stories about near-death experiences with a child, when he or she is old enough to comprehend them, is a great way to reassure a child that death isn't final and that the soul is infinite. For psychic kids, stories about NDEs can also help to confirm that their experiences with the dead are real and valid.

A SENSE OF COMMUNITY IS VITAL

Feeling that he can share his paranormal experiences with an adult who will believe and accept them can go a long way toward keeping a psychic child from feeling overwhelmed. I've found over the years that the majority of these young people are extremely well grounded, socially adept, articulate, and talented in many ways that have nothing to do with their psychic abilities. They may be good at sports, art, music, or any number of things, but when the psychic experiences they're having get out of control, they may become all-encompassing and overshadow all the other aspects of their lives.

In fact, Karen, from the story earlier, told me that up to the point when, at about age thirteen, Linda began to have paranormal experiences, she had been a very outgoing and social little girl. But as she became more and more overwhelmed by what was coming at her from the spirit world, she also started to become more and more withdrawn. Having finally opened up to her daughter about her own psychic experiences, Karen hoped that knowing she had an understanding confidant in her mother would help to lift Linda's burden and allow her to reclaim her own joy in life.

It's important for everyone to find a community of like-minded, understanding individuals, but for psychic kids, who often feel marginalized and who may have been victimized, discovering that there are other kids like them can be literally life-changing.

Some of the reasons the kids on our program come in pairs or groups is that the experience is less overwhelming when they're with others approximately their own age. It's also validating and reassuring for them to know that the other children are picking up many of the same things they are, and—perhaps most important—it gives them the opportunity to meet and talk freely with others who are like them.

In chapter 1 we met Brad C.; Brad's sister, Morgan; and Joel, who appeared on the same episode. Brad, as I said, was having some difficulty understanding and accepting his gift, and Joel was frightened by the spirits he'd been seeing. As it happens, Brad and Joel were approximately the same age, and meeting each other had a remarkably positive effect on both of them. Many of the psychic kids I've met and worked with have never met another child with psychic abilities. They're struggling to make sense of what's happening to them and why, and they often feel extremely isolated, alone, and freakish. They've described themselves to me as weird, outcast, different, not fitting in, afraid, crazy, sick, and delusional. One girl had even had the word "witch" scrawled on her school locker. Therefore, it's very important for them to know that there are other kids like them and that they are not as alone as they might think.

Unfortunately, Western culture has not yet embraced psychic kids and their gifts to the degree other cultures have done. In China, psychic kids are sought out and sent to special schools where their talents can be studied and developed—in much the same way that talented ice skaters or gymnasts are sought out and supported from a very early age.

These groups of "super psychic" children, as they are called, have demonstrated amazing abilities, including the ability to read with body parts other than their eyes and using telekinesis to move objects with their minds. These children were first discovered in 1974 and were carefully scrutinized by both the Chinese government and the scientific community. By the mid-1980s, China had established training facilities to assist these youngsters in developing their psychic abilities, and by 1997 at least a hundred thousand of these super psychic children had been identified. More than a thousand similar children have also been identified in Mexico.

In England, there is a school called Arthur Findlay College that is devoted to the study of spiritualism. But in the United States there are extremely limited resources available for nurturing and developing psychic talents. There is no Hogwarts, no institution devoted to educating young "wizards."

In Durham, North Carolina, the Rhine Research Center, which grew out of the Parapsychology Laboratory at Duke University founded by J. B. Rhine in the late 1930s, is devoted to studying the nature and enhancement of consciousness. And at the University of Arizona, Professor Gary Schwartz is directing ongoing research into the survival of consciousness after physical death. Valuable as these programs are, however, they do not answer the needs of children and young people in the process of coming to terms with their psychic gifts. There are a few summer camps for psychic kids, but these resources are still few and far between.

To answer that need, I've established a message board located at http://chipcoffey.proboards.com/index.cgi? as a safe place for everyone, including psychic kids, to discuss and share their experiences. The discussions are moderated by two talented and responsible psychics who make sure that the messages are kept safe for kids and do not offend or impinge upon anyone's personal religious or spiritual beliefs. That said, I should also make it clear that the opinions expressed by those who moderate the board, as well as those who post there, do not necessarily reflect my own opinions and beliefs.

Many of those who come to my message board also send private messages to the moderators or to me asking for personal advice or information related to their own psychic experiences and abilities.

In addition, I've found that many of the young people who appeared on *Psychic Kids* have reached out to one another and formed a community among themselves. Many have gained enough confidence in themselves to establish an online presence through social networking sites such as Facebook where other kids can communicate and connect with them.

Now I'm hoping that *Growing Up Psychic* will become another tool kids can use not only to read about other psychic kids but also to educate themselves. One of my purposes in writing this book is to provide information to the thousands of psychic kids and their parents whom I can't contact personally with detailed answers to the many questions they post on my message board and to let them know that they are not alone. If you are a psychic kid reading this book, I want you to know that there are thousands of others like you, and you, too, should be proud rather than afraid or ashamed of your gift.

GAINING CONTROL IS KEY

All psychic kids need to understand that they can take control of what they receive from the world of spirit so that it doesn't take over and impinge upon every other aspect of their lives. They need to feel that they are in charge so that they don't feel victimized. They need to know that being psychic is not a curse and that they can learn to consciously tap into their paranormal abilities at will rather than have psychic experiences occurring spontaneously, unsolicited, and as uninvited, unwanted invasions of their lives.

In *Black Swan* and the much earlier film *The Red Shoes* we saw fictional representations of what can happen when people who are unusually gifted (in these stories ballerinas) are consumed by their gifts and their lives spiral out of control. While neither film claims to be an accurate portrayal of actual events, their dramatic license drives home the necessity for any gifted individual to take control of the talent that might otherwise take control of him.

No one wants to feel helpless, hopeless, and unable to cope. (And many kids, psychic or not, tend to feel that way a lot of the time.) Psychic children need to be as normal as possible. Being psychic is only one part of who they are, and they can't be "psychic kids" 24/7. They also need to go to school, do homework, participate in sports and social events, go on trips, and hang out with friends, just like any other kid. They need to become well-rounded people.

Many things came together to allow me to do what I do, and most of them are not related to being psychic. I was a child actor, which taught me not only to be comfortable interacting with other people but also how to navigate my way around a television studio. I also studied traditional counseling, which taught me how to understand people on a human psychological level. And working in the travel industry taught me how to travel comfortably, which has now allowed me to "take my show on the road" so to speak and go from place to place with a minimum of stress. All of these are pieces of the puzzle that have led to my being able to earn a living as a psychic. And now, when I do a reading for someone, it very often sounds more like a therapy session than a psychic reading. What I tell people may sound more like good common sense than some kind of divine wisdom received from above, and, in fact, the information I impart very often is about daily life skills and better decision-making. The reason for this, I believe, is that my spirit guides are very aware of who I am as a person, and they utilize my real-world skills and experiences when they deliver information to me to pass on to my clients. They also know my personality and show me images that they know will resonate with me. As an example, when I'm doing a reading for someone who is clearly in need of a wake-up call to figure out how he's been messing up and getting in his own way, Wesley, one of my spirit guides, will show me the scene in the movie *Moonstruck* where Cher smacks Nicolas Cage and tells him sternly to "snap out of it."

Whatever a psychic kid does and learns in other aspects of his life will ultimately contribute to his being a better psychic. And whether or not he ultimately decides to make his gift his vocation, he still needs to develop all aspects of himself and become the best person he can be.

When I talk to the children on *Psychic Kids*, I see how their attitude and outlook change the minute they begin to understand that they can control when and where they tap into their psychic abilities. When I ask them to concentrate, focus, and tell me what they're sensing, and when I can then validate that what they're pulling in is accurate, they almost immediately shift from feeling beleaguered to feeling empowered. They feel—sometimes for the first time—awesome rather than afraid.

CALL ON YOUR ANGELS AND SPIRIT GUIDES

Time and time again, I am asked, "How can I learn to manage my psychic abilities?" There is no one specific way to gain more control that works for everyone. The process for doing so is very individualistic. One woman I know says that putting on a baseball cap keeps spirits from communicating with her uninvited. Some people have told me they wear earplugs to block out unwanted energies and communication. But the primary way I suggest that psychic kids (and adults) can take charge of their abilities is to ask their spirit guides, their guardian angels, or God to intervene and help manage the inflow of information.

Being psychic is a divine gift, and it's perfectly appropriate, therefore, to ask for divine help in managing what we've been given. Even though I never had to consciously work at learning how to access my abilities, I did—and still do—call upon my angels and spirit guides to help me gain control of what is coming at me. I like to tell people that I never wanted to be Whoopi Goldberg in the movie *Ghost*, with spirits surrounding me at all hours of the day and night. And, beyond that, I don't want to be trespassing on other people's private business by spontaneously receiving information about everyone with whom I come into contact on a daily basis.

I met the entities with whom I still work most closely many years ago in very sad circumstances. My dog, Barney, had just died suddenly at the age of three, and I was totally grief stricken. On the day he died I was with a very spiritual friend who took me to a park and told me that I was about to meet my angels and guides. She took me through a guided meditation, and on that terrible, sad, and traumatic afternoon, sitting in the bright sunshine, I met seven spirits who gave me their names and who remain my spiritual support team, protectors, and friends to this day.

Early in our relationship, my spirit guide Wesley described himself to me as resembling the outspoken, outlandish character Jack McFarland on the popular sitcom *Will & Grace*, and although that description was, initially, somewhat off-putting, I've come to know him as someone who doesn't mince words, always tells it like it is, and has a great, acerbic sense of humor. I'm convinced that if we were living on this planet at the same time we'd be the best of friends.

I believe we all have spirit guides and guardian angels who partner with us for various purposes and reasons. They seem to come when we need them most. Here is one of the most amazing angelic manifestations I've ever personally experienced. My mother had been living with me for several years after my father died when, one New Year's Eve, she became very ill and was admitted to the cardiac intensive care unit of our local hospital. The prognosis was grim and I was advised that she might not make it through the night. Needless to say, I was devastated.

She was assigned a handsome male nurse who introduced himself as Micah and told her that he'd be taking care of her. When he saw how frightened and upset I was, he gently suggested that I go home and try to get some rest. When I protested that I needed to be there with my mother, he said, "I promise that I'll take good care of her. If we need you, I'll call you."

For whatever reason, I trusted him. I went home and lay down on the living room sofa with the cordless phone clutched in my hand. When I awoke early the next morning, it hadn't rung. I called the hospital and was assured that my mother was resting comfortably. When I got there, she told me what had happened after I left. Micah had come in to check on her. When he asked how she was feeling, she said, "I think I'm going to die tonight." "No, you're not," he said. "No one is allowed to die on my watch." She told me that she'd felt calm, peaceful, and safe for the rest of the night. "You're going to think I'm crazy," she told me, "but there was a thin silver cord coming out of this finger"— she held up the ring finger on her right hand—"and it was somehow attached to Micah. I knew everything he was doing, everywhere he went. He was sending me powerful energy, and I believe he kept me alive."

Somewhere deep in my soul I knew she was right. Micah had kept her alive through that dark night and into the New Year. When she was released from the hospital several days later, I went back to the cardiac care unit to thank Micah one more time. When I spoke to the nurse on duty, she told me something that gave me chills. Micah had not shown up for work in two or three days. The phone number on his employment application had been disconnected, and, in fact, he'd worked there for only a few days before my mother was admitted.

As I thanked the nurse and left the unit my mind was racing. Could Micah have been a guardian angel sent to watch over my mother and me? I've always felt a special bond with the archangel Michael, and I believe that God sent one of His most divine helpers to us in our time of need.

So, yes, our guardian angels and spirit guides do manifest when we need them most, but we can also call upon them at will once we open our hearts and minds and learn how to access their energy. We can reach out and seek the connection by focusing our intention on making it happen. The classic way to do this is through meditation, but, frankly, I find that I simply can't slow my brain down enough to get into a meditative state. And, beyond that, I'm now over fifty years old and if I ever managed to get into a lotus position I'd probably be stuck there for the rest of my life. What I do instead is to set apart a period of time each day to just "be." I allow myself a few minutes of quiet reflection to let my mind roam freely and receive anything that might come to me. That's my form of meditation.

I tell people—psychic kids included—if you can get into the classic meditative zone, great! If not, just take some time to take a nap, go for a walk, sit down and close your eyes for a few minutes, get out in nature—whatever it takes to put you into a receptive state of mind—and invite your guides in the world of spirit to make themselves known.

On one episode of *Psychic Kids*, Jordi had been sensing a male presence in her room at night. When she told me about it, she said she was frightened even though the entity hadn't done anything that was in any way threatening. As we talked I was able to tap into that energy, and I told her that I believed the presence she was feeling was an angel or spirit guide who was there to protect rather than prey upon her. I was even able to provide her with a name—Jonathan. After being quiet for a moment, Jordi smiled and told me that felt right to her and that the spirit was being sort of sarcastic about the fact that I'd said it was a nice name. So I suggested that she attempt to converse with Jonathan either telepathically or out loud in order to open up a channel of communication and establish a relationship with him. Jordi later reported to me that she and Jonathan were in the process of finding ways to work effectively together by connecting spirit energy with human energy.

The process of creating that connection with one's spirit guides is so personal that there isn't really a one-size-fits-all formula for how to do it. That said, however, everyone can do it; it's just a matter of finding the way that's best suited to each individual. I always tell people that it may take some patience; if one thing doesn't work, try another, and don't get impatient—which can be difficult in a world where we've come to expect instant gratification.

As I told a young girl named Riley, who confessed on one episode of *Psychic Kids* that she was sometimes frightened by the spiritual information coming at her unbidden, I don't want kids to be afraid of paranormal experiences. I want them to take charge of when and where they receive psychic information (so that they don't, as I like to put it, become Western Union messengers for the dead). To do that, I help them to connect with their spirit guides, but I also tell them that they can use their most authoritative voice to tell spirits who are coming at them unbidden to simply go away. No one has any obligation to become the involuntary messenger for those in spirit, and, in my experience, most spirits will respect those boundaries.

But I also don't want kids to run away from their ability. I want them to understand that it comes with the responsibility to use it wisely for the greater good. I want them to honor and respect the gift that's been bestowed upon them. And the better they are able to control it, the more they will see it as a blessing.

CHECKLIST FOR PARENTS

- Make it clear to your child that "psychic" is not a synonym for "omniscient."
- Make it safe for your child to discuss his paranormal experiences with you.
- Let him know if you, too, have had paranormal experiences.
- Explain death and dying on a level your child can understand.

- Help him to connect with a community of other psychic kids with whom he can share his experiences.

- Do what you can to validate his experiences so that he can see them as a gift.

- Urge him to connect with his spirit guides and guardian angels for guidance and protection.

CHAPTER FOUR

The Need for Psychic Protection

Being able to control your gift and manage your psychic abilities is also a way to protect yourself from taking on unwanted energy and having your life intruded upon by negative or malevolent entities.

Yes, it's true. There are bullies and meanies in the spirit world just as there are in the schoolyard. Most of us would not think twice about stepping in to protect a child from a schoolyard bully, and that should hold true for psychic bullies as well.

On the first episode of our third season of *Psychic Kids*, there was a young boy named Nick who was being harassed by a malevolent spirit named Mr. Rosenberg. At the time, Nick was a well-spoken, all-American eleven-year-old with dark hair and bright blue eyes. He had moved with his parents from California to Ohio, and one day when he was taking a shortcut through a local cemetery, as he often did on his way home from school, Mr. Rosenberg followed him and began to threaten him and command him to do things he didn't want to do. From then on, he started to harass Nick on a regular basis. One night, he got so angry that he physically threw Nick out of his bed. When the poor embattled boy came to us he was understandably terrified, but during the time we spent together, we empowered him to banish Mr. Rosenberg forever. We all got together—Nick and his parents, the other child on the program and her mother, Edy Nathan, and I—and each of us in turn told Mr. Rosenberg in no uncertain terms to leave Nick alone. After the rest of us had each taken a turn, Nick repeated, loud and clear, "*I want you to leave me alone. You're not allowed to touch me or hurt me or bother me ever again,*" and then he burst into tears. When I asked him what he was feeling, he said, "He left," at which point all of us were in tears. It was a beautiful moment.

When I tell people Nick's story they very often ask me if it's possible for a ghost to follow you home from a haunted location. The answer is that it doesn't happen very often, but it is possible, and, in fact, it has happened to me.

I'm aware that some aspects of the following story may be disturbing to some people. But this is the way it happened, the details are part of our cultural history, and—unfortunately—we can't rewrite history; we can only hope to learn from it.

A few years ago I was asked to consult on a case for a woman I'll call Kate and her daughter, whom I'll call Taylor, who had recently moved into a historic home and almost immediately began to have weird experiences, such as power outages that were not caused by anything in the electrical system. They also told me about an even more troubling event. During a recent rainstorm water had begun pouring through their roof, and when Kate called in a repairman, he told her that the shingles had been totally ripped off the roof, even though there had been no tornado or damaging winds in the area. The repairman placed tarps on the roof until he could make the necessary repairs, and Kate went off to the shop she owned in town, which she was stunned to find was also completely flooded. At that point she was at her wit's end—but there was more. When she went back out to her car, it too was flooded. Yes, it was still raining, and yes, her car was a convertible, but the roof was up, all the windows were shut, and there was absolutely no way that much water could have gotten inside the car.

Kate was fairly convinced that something paranormal was occurring and determined to find out what was going on, so she went to the town historian to see if she could gather any information about the history of the house. Here's what she found out. In the early 1900s, the house was occupied by a fairly affluent family who had a teenage daughter. There was a young African-American man who did general handyman work for the family and with whom the daughter was secretly having an affair. The daughter got pregnant and when her parents found out they lynched the handyman and threw his body into the river. As the story went, all this was unspoken common knowledge at the time, although, of course, back in the day, it was put forth that the handyman had committed suicide by drowning himself.

The first time I went to Kate's home I knew nothing about its tragic history. When I did my initial walk-through, I felt the presence of several spirits, including an older man, a young Caucasian female, and a very angry African-American male.

One of the first things I do when I go to a client's home is, as I've said, look at what's on the bookshelves. In this case I found in the daughter's room a book about how to be a teenage witch as well as the entire *Twilight* series of fantasy novels featuring vampires and werewolves, and the mother had books about Wicca as well as books on how to cast spells. It was clear to me that they had an avid interest in the supernatural and that this made them perfect candidates for having paranormal experiences.

After I completed my walk-through, Kate and I sat down to talk about my psychic impressions and she shared with me the information she had learned about the history of her home. We decided that it would be a good idea to bring in a team of paranormal investigators and do a full-scale investigation of the house.

When I got back home that afternoon, I took my usual afternoon nap, and when I awoke, I heard an unusual hissing noise. As I followed the sound into the back hallway, I found myself ankle-deep in water that was pouring out of my hot water heater. I turned off the water under the house and called Mr. Jackson, my plumber, to make an emergency visit. When he took a look at the heater he was flabbergasted. Both the intake and the outflow valves had blown simultaneously, which, Mr. Jackson informed me, almost never happens.

I had already begun to suspect that Kate's water issues were related to the murdered handyman whose body was thrown into a river, who, I believed, was manifesting as a water poltergeist. Now it seemed that he was annoyed with me as well and had followed me home.

In any case, Mr. Jackson brought me a new water heater and as he was installing it he asked if I had any idea how my previous water heater could have blown both valves at once. Since he was already familiar with my work (and sometimes liked to tease me by calling me Mr. Ghost Buster), I decided to tell him the whole story. When I got done, he just shook his head and said, "You know, I've learned in my life never to think that anything is impossible." And then he asked, "Would you like me to talk to that ghost?" So Mr. Jackson, who is African-American, started to speak: "If there's the spirit of a young black man in this house that's bothering Mr. Coffey, I just want you to know this. He's a good man. He's not like those other men who hurt you. Look at me, I'm a black man, too, and he treats me with kindness and respect. I'm doing work for him and he's paying me good money for my work, but Mr. Coffey is also my friend, and I'm going to ask you as one black man to another to just leave him alone and not bother him anymore."

I was really touched by that, and I thanked him profusely, and I never had any further problems with that ghost.

Of course, that didn't really help Kate and Taylor, but we did finish our investigation and performed various cleansing rituals, and when we were done we advised them to be prudent about any spell work or witchcraft they might be doing because they could be opening doors to paranormal activity that might then be very difficult to close.

MOST SPIRITS MEAN NO HARM

Not all bothersome spirits are evil or malevolent. Most, in fact, are completely harmless. Some are simply stuck and unable to move on to the higher plane, and some who may at first appear to be malicious—particularly to a young person who doesn't know what to make of his or her psychic intercommunications—are actually benevolent. Remember that Jordi was initially frightened of the spirit entity she felt in her bedroom until she learned that it was actually a spirit guide who was there to protect her. Every bump or groan you hear in your house does not mean that you're going to be reliving the Amityville horror. It could simply be your grandma coming to check on you or someone who's lived in your house in the past dropping by for a visit.

EVIL DOES EXIST

That said, however, it is important to remember that the "landscape" of the paranormal is a vastly unknown and uncharted territory and one can never be certain of what (or who) is going to come through.

Most people who have passed into the world of spirit will continue to evolve and grow—assuming that they're willing to participate in the process. But just as some of us on earth learn less quickly than others, so do some spirits hang on to their negative characteristics and habits longer than others. For that reason, it is generally not a good idea to taunt or provoke any supernatural entity, because one can never be certain of how the spirit will react. I'm not suggesting that anyone should live in fear of the paranormal, but it is seldom a bad idea to err on the side of caution when dealing with anything we do not fully understand.

If for no other reason it is therefore always important for the parents of psychic children to make them feel safe and protected.

Young psychics, who may not yet be fully in control of their abilities or their reactions, may get into potentially dangerous psychic situations. They could, for example, fall prey to a malicious or malevolent spirit, as Nick did with Mr. Rosenberg. Or they could become the victim of a demonic entity. A demon, to my mind, is the evil counterpart of an angel. In biblical terms, a demon is a fallen angel, which means that it has never had human form. At some point, the story goes, there was a war in heaven, and Lucifer, the most beautiful of all the angels, led an uprising, attempting to overthrow God. An army of "good" angels, led by the archangel Michael, vanquished Lucifer, who, along with his followers, was banished to hell.

One child named Tammy who appeared on the program said that every time she looked in a mirror she saw a demon, and consequently, all the mirrors in her house were covered and she hadn't looked at her own reflection in years—until we supported her while making her look in the mirror and showing her that she had the power to banish her demon forever.

WHAT ABOUT DEMONIC POSSESSION?

I was recently contacted by the parents of a teenage girl whom they believe to be possessed. Among the disturbing behaviors they'd noticed were that she'd been walking around as if in a fugue state, losing periods of time, distancing herself from family and friends, appearing to be depressed and anxious, talking in a strange guttural tone, and experiencing radical changes in her eating habits. Her father is a medical doctor who had put her through a complete physical workup, including every test available to explain her symptoms, and she'd also been evaluated by a psychiatrist. But there was nothing on any CT scan or MRI, nothing in the *Diagnostic and Statistical Manual,* and no changes in the circumstances of her daily life that could reasonably account for all the symptoms she was experiencing. When the father called me, he was at his wit's end and told me that, hard as it was for him, he had no choice but to believe that his child was under spiritual or demonic attack. Feeling completely hopeless and helpless, the family contacted their local Catholic archdiocese and requested that an exorcism be performed on their child. As I am writing this book, the parents are awaiting approval from their bishop for the exorcism to take place.

POSSIBLE WARNING SIGNS OF DEMONIC POSSESSION

The belief in demonic possession—that is, a person's falling under the control of one or more malevolent spiritual entities—has existed among various cultures and religions since ancient times.

In the early 1970s, William Peter Blatty's novel *The Exorcist* and the film based on it shocked the world with their graphic depictions of a young girl named Regan who was possessed by the devil and the exorcism performed on her by two Catholic priests. Since that time, there have been numerous other movies and television shows about possession and exorcism.

In 2005 and again in 2011, the Vatican responded to the dramatic increase in the number of reported possible possessions and requests for exorcisms by training hundreds of priests worldwide in the rites of exorcism at seminars held in Rome, and in 2010, the Church also conducted training sessions for new exorcists in the United States.

Evidently, the Catholic Church considers possession to be a serious concern that is reaching epidemic proportions and is therefore preparing its priests for spiritual warfare. But exorcisms are not performed solely by Catholics; clergy from other Christian and non-Christian religions have begun performing them on a frequent basis.

Although I believe that it's wise to use great caution when looking for information on the Internet, I think that the following, from the Foundation for the Study of Paranormal Phenomena, provides some accurate warning signs of demonic possession or oppression. What follows is a partial list I've adapted from that site. For a complete list you can go to http://fspp.net/warn%20poss.htm. But also remember the caveat on the website that states, "What follows is a guide; it can help you to make a determination whether there is a psychiatric problem or a demonic one. However, it is not the end all. One should not read an article on brain tumors and diagnose themselves as having one. Neither should they look at this article and decide they are possessed by an evil entity."

MENTAL CHANGES AFFECTING THE PERSON

- Changes in personality. This is usually seen when the person is affable and suddenly becomes extremely quiet.
- Someone who is normally very active suddenly becomes isolated.
- Changes in sleep patterns.
- Sudden weight loss or gain.

- Changes in attitude and behavior, usually becoming hostile.
- Suddenly beginning to curse a lot when that is out of character.
- Developing a sudden aversion to religious objects or observance, or suddenly destroying religious objects.
- Beginning to collect occult materials.
- Evidence of self-mutilation.
- Suddenly becoming abusive or threatening to others or attempting to hurt animals.
- Changes in personal hygiene.
- Experiencing severe nightmares or night terrors.
- Performing acts of humiliation, such as urinating on themselves, etc.
- Excessive masturbation or doing it in front of others.
- Appearing to have multiple personalities.
- Unusual changes in diet or food preferences.
- Having blackouts or episodes of memory loss.

PHYSICAL CHANGES AFFECTING THE PERSON

- Going for long periods of time without blinking.
- Appearing catatonic.
- Becoming completely rigid and unmovable, even by multiple people.
- Suddenly seeming to possess inhuman strength.
- Speaking a language the person could not possibly know, speaking English with an unusual accent, or speaking in tongues.

- Changes in hair color or the eyes, which may turn extremely black.
- Obvious changes in facial features.
- Changes in voice, which may go from high to low to guttural.
- Speaking in multiple voices.
- Moving in some unusual way, such as gliding instead of walking.
- Writing or symbols appearing on the body in the form of welts and scratches, especially in areas the person could not reach.
- Levitating.

Having said all that, however, I must emphasize once again that if a child (or adult) is having paranormal experiences, it should never be automatically assumed that he is possessed by an evil spirit or mentally ill. He may be psychic and totally sane (as is most often the case), psychic and mentally ill, psychic and possessed, or mentally ill and believing he's possessed when he's not. There are many fine lines here that can become entangled and difficult to unravel. And sometimes it can be hard to differentiate one from the other(s).

Several years ago, I met a woman who shared a very bizarre, but also very true, story with me. Her family had once suffered from what she now believes to have been a demonic oppression that focused strongly on her young daughter. That, in itself, was a compelling tale, but the story became even more twisted when she revealed that its cast of characters also included music icon John Lennon and Mark David Chapman, the man who murdered Lennon. I have included this story, entitled "With a Little Help from My Friends: Did Demons Force Mark David Chapman to Murder John Lennon?" in appendix B.

KIDS NEED TO LEARN TO DIFFERENTIATE THE GOOD FROM THE BENIGN AND THE UGLY

It is important to be wary of any psychic or similar "spiritual practitioner" who announces that you or your child is "cursed" or "possessed" or "under an evil spell" and claims that he or she can remove the curse of the spell—for a price. These charlatans are much more likely to rid you of your hard-earned cash than of any evil entity.

Nevertheless, all psychic kids (and their parents) do need to learn how to tell the difference between benign or benevolent spirits and those who are harmful. Chances are, when bothersome or even malicious paranormal activity is occurring, the offending entity is simply a nasty-tempered human spirit, not a demon. It is also vital for them to learn what they need to do to get evil entities out of their lives. When they're confronted by a malevolent spirit, they need to be strong, stand up for themselves, and demand that the spirit leave them alone, much as they would with someone who was bothering or bullying them in life. When it comes to dealing with a harmful spirit, kids need to know that they have that strength and the ability to use it.

If a child is having experiences he doesn't understand or feels the need to protect himself, and if he doesn't know where to go for the help or the information he is seeking, he may turn to unreliable Internet sites, books, or other sources that may misinform him and put him in even greater danger. One child, who appeared on the program with Olivia S., said that she thought she was an "empath." And another, named Haley, had a mirror in her room that she and her mother had bought at a yard sale and Haley said she believed was a "portal" used by spirits to contact her. To me, the fact that these were not terms kids normally encounter in the course of conversation meant that they must have been doing some research on their own.

While I believe very strongly that psychics need to educate themselves about what they're experiencing, the problem with this kind of "private investigation" is that it can create more problems than it solves and make kids even more frightened than they already are. If, for example, they Google "psychic kids" what they're likely to come up with is a variety of sites talking about crystal and indigo children who have been put on earth to save or change the world. And that would be a heavy burden for any kid—much less one who is already feeling beleaguered by his or her difference—to carry. My goal has been and will always be to make psychic kids feel more normal, not more confused or crazier than they already feel.

One of my missions, therefore, is to make sure these kids have a person or an information source (including this book) that will be accurate, truly helpful, and well intended. That, in addition to creating a sense of community, is one of the primary purposes of my message board.

PROTECTION YOU CAN USE

There are rituals and rites anyone can perform to protect himself and his environment from being invaded by unwelcome spirits. Many of them have been used since ancient times and may vary depending on the culture and belief system by which they were created. I believe strongly that we all need to believe in something that makes us feel safe and secure and cling to that belief. If a faith-based belief system works for you, that's great, but you need to believe in *something* that is protective, beneficent, and benevolent, even if it's only the power of goodness and light.

One of the most frightening, yet hopeful, stories that I have ever heard about demonic infestation was told to me by Carmen Snedecker (who now goes by her maiden name, Carmen Reed). Carmen and her family had recently moved into a small house in Southington, Connecticut, when she made a shocking discovery in the basement. Partially hidden under building and construction materials, she found tools and equipment typically used by morticians. The house they were occupying had previously been a funeral home.

Before long, strange and frightening things began to happen. One day, as Carmen was mopping the kitchen floor, the water suddenly turned blood red and had a terrible odor. Crucifixes hanging throughout the house began to disappear. Carmen's niece, who was living with the family, was physically assaulted in her sleep by unseen hands that groped and grabbed at her body. A rosary she had placed around her neck was violently yanked by the abusive entity and the beads scattered all across the floor.

In the weeks that followed several demonic entities made their evil presence known. "They were incredibly powerful," Carmen said. "One of the demons was very thin, with high cheekbones, long black hair, and pitch-black eyes. Another had white hair and eyes and wore a pinstriped tuxedo, and his feet were constantly in motion."

Her formerly "preppy" oldest son soon began wearing only dark clothing and suffered dramatic personality changes. He became increasingly angry and violent and he started writing dark, disturbing poetry.

The family frequently smelled foul odors in the house, including the scents of rotting flesh and excrement. At one point, a dark mist enveloped Carmen and her niece while they were together in the kitchen, disorienting and paralyzing both of them. Terrified, Carmen began to recite the Lord's Prayer and the demon released them.

Desperate, Carmen telephoned renowned paranormal experts Ed and Lorraine Warren and begged them for help. Ed, Lorraine, and their team of investigators literally moved into the Snedeckers' home for an astounding nine weeks in order to witness for themselves all the supernatural events that were allegedly occurring.

John Zaffis, Ed's nephew, who was a member of the investigative team, remembers that shortly after arriving, members of the team began to be "touched" by the entities. He also remembers the vile odors that frequently permeated the house. "One night," he said, "I was sitting at the dining room table, reviewing some notes that I'd made. Suddenly, the room grew bitterly cold and I could sense a presence around me. I called out to the others, who were sleeping in the living room, but I couldn't get anyone to wake up. I looked up the stairs and saw an apparition starting to form. The air was filled with a disgusting odor, so foul that I could hardly breathe. As the apparition took shape, I could hear a noise that sounded like thousands of flapping wings coming from behind it. I'd never been more terrified in my life!"

Finally, the decision was made to conduct an exorcism on the house. Following the ritual, "the house definitely felt lighter and we all felt a sense of calm and relief," Zaffis recalled.

It has now been more than two decades since these events took place. Since that time, Carmen has been "approached" by negative forces, and she firmly believes that is it her unwavering faith and unflinching courage that have kept the evil energies at bay.

I firmly believe that with any kind of ritual, it is the intent with which it is used that affects the energy it creates. Whatever makes you most comfortable is what you should use. I myself am a very strong proponent of trying everything positive until something works. Here are a few protective mechanisms that have proved to be powerful over time:

Smudging: This is a Native American ritual using sage or sweetgrass. It's done in honor of the four elements—earth, air, fire, and water. The sage or sweetgrass represents earth; lighting it represents fire; fanning the smoke with a bird feather represents air; storing the sage in a shell taken from the sea represents water. If you are smudging your house or property, you need to remember to do it in all areas (including the basement, the attic, and the closets) and all four corners, facing in all four directions (east, west, north, and south).

Blessed/Sacred Objects: Many people use iconic religious objects such as crosses or religious medals, a *chai* or a Star of David, a hand of Fatima, an ankh, or an eye of Horus to protect against evil spirits. Native Americans will often wear a medicine bag around their neck. Some people wear or carry crystals. Some, for example, wear jewelry made of hematite, a mineral with magnetic properties, to absorb negative energies. (I wear blessed holy medals at all times, which drove the sound technicians crazy when we were filming *Psychic Kids* until they figured out they could tape them together so that they didn't clink when I was miked.)

Creating a Protective Circle: Some people encircle their property with salt, which has been used for centuries as a protective element, or with holy water. If I had a Native American name it would probably be "Travels with Holy Water," because I never leave home without it.

Prayer: If you believe in the world of spirit, it seems to me that you must also believe there is some higher entity or "force" at work in the universe. No matter what your religious belief (or lack thereof), praying is one of the most powerful ways to protect yourself from any kind of negative energy or spirit.

KNOWLEDGE IS POWER

I want to reiterate here that the vast majority of spirits do not intend anyone any harm, but that doesn't mean we want them interrupting our everyday lives whenever they feel like paying a call. Therefore, the more psychic kids—and adults—know about their own empowerment, including the power of protection, the more in control they will feel, the more comfortable they will be with their gifts, and the better able they will be to use them wisely and effectively.

CHECKLIST FOR PARENTS

- Understand that most spirits are benign but that bullies and meanies do exist in the world of spirit.
- Never discount what your child might tell you about feeling harassed or endangered by a spirit entity.
- Learn to recognize the signs of demonic possession.
- Teach your child the protective rituals and mechanisms he can use to keep himself safe.

CHAPTER FIVE

Dealing with Skeptics and Disbelievers

I gnorance abounds in every segment of society. People tend to fear whatever is unfamiliar or what they don't understand. Here is a prime example of how destructive ignorance can be—and the healing powers of acceptance.

Cooper, a sweet, sensitive little guy who appeared on the pilot for our program, had made the mistake of telling his kindergarten teacher that he saw dead people. As a result, he was taken out of his class and kept sequestered in a separate room where a teacher worked with him one-on-one. He wasn't allowed to have any interaction with any of the other children for two entire years. During that time, his mother, Kelly, took him to a psychiatrist, who put him on medication.

Cooper had been saying that after his grandmother died she had been coming to him, and she was delivering messages about things he couldn't possibly have known. Once Kelly was able to verify the information Cooper had been relaying to her from his grandmother, she realized that he'd been telling the truth, and, at that point, she took him off the drugs and demanded that he be mainstreamed and returned to the classroom.

In another, equally unfortunate case, a boy named Bryson who appeared on an episode of *Psychic Kids* was actually sent to a mental institution because he said he saw spirits. When Bryson was about four years old, he told his mother, Judi, that he was "seeing people" in his room at night. Initially, Judi wasn't too concerned, thinking these "people" were just creations of Bryson's childhood imagination. Later, however, when he was in fifth grade, he began exhibiting signs of stress and throwing up in school. He was hospitalized and underwent a series of tests, but the only diagnosis the doctors could come up with was that he was having anxiety attacks.

Unbeknownst to Judi, Bryson was again "seeing people," and by this time he had figured out that they were dead! He went to his school counselor to tell her what was happening and added, "I just want all of this to end." What the counselor took from this was that Bryson was at risk for suicide and crying out for help.

The counselor phoned Judi and told her that she should immediately take Bryson to the emergency room. Frightened for her son's safety, Judi followed the counselor's instructions. At the local children's hospital, Bryson was kept in a room with a guard at the door until a state mental health worker arrived several hours later. When the mental health worker asked Bryson if he could see and hear people no one else heard or saw, he told her there was another person in the room with them at that very moment. Upon hearing this, Judi suddenly came to a startling realization.

She remembered that her grandmother, her mother, and, as a young girl, even she had had paranormal experiences. "I immediately knew that this was what was happening to Bryson. But how could I explain it to his doctors? They would never have believed me, and I was certain that Bryson would be diagnosed as suffering from schizophrenia," Judi told me. She decided not to say anything, but, in the end, it didn't matter.

The mental health worker had Bryson sedated and transferred by ambulance, at four o'clock in the morning, to the state mental hospital many miles away, where he was placed on a seventy-two-hour hold for observation. At the state hospital he was kept behind locked doors with the windows blacked out. When Judi was finally allowed to see him, she said it was "like visiting a prisoner" and she was horrified by what she discovered. "Bryson was so drugged up that he was barely coherent." After three days she demanded that he be released. Again, the only diagnosis was an anxiety disorder.

Before Bryson was allowed to return to school, Judi was required to meet with school officials, including the principal, the guidance counselor, his teachers, and the school psychologist. They told Judi that they believed it was in Bryson's best interest not to return to school and offered to provide a tutor to teach Bryson at home. When Judi inquired as to why the officials had made this decision, she was told they considered Bryson to be a threat to the other students.

Judi informed them that this was not acceptable, so as an alternative, they offered to place Bryson in a special education class. She agreed, feeling that he might receive some extra attention in a smaller, more specialized classroom environment. But, several days after Bryson returned to school, Judi visited him in the special education classroom and quickly realized that this was not where her child needed to be. She immediately withdrew Bryson from public school and began homeschooling him, which she continues to do even today.

As of this writing, Bryson is fifteen years old, and Judi described him to me as socially well-adjusted, loving, affectionate, and mature beyond his years. He is no longer ashamed and is much less afraid of what he experiences, and he continues to learn how to deal with whatever comes up. She also wanted me to know that his experience with *Psychic Kids* had been very positive and had provided both her and Bryson with coping skills that serve them well to this day.

Judi is willing to share this story publicly because she knows that other children and parents are going through situations similar to those that she and Bryson endured. "Both Bryson and I hope that hearing our story will help others to find their own courage and strength," she said.

Sadly, stories like those of Cooper and Bryson are not uncommon. I have met numerous other psychic kids who have been similarly treated by teachers, counselors, and mental health professionals. Many individuals whom we trust to educate, counsel, and care for our children have never encountered a psychic child and may misunderstand, misdiagnose, and mistreat them out of ignorance. Or they may misjudge children who claim to have psychic abilities or paranormal experiences simply because they are unwilling to accept the possibility that these types of phenomena are real and valid.

Skeptics are all around us, and, personally, I don't normally try to defend what I do or attempt to make believers of doubters. At this point in my life, there's not much people could say that would hurt me, and there's certainly nothing they could say to make me doubt myself. But it's taken a while for me to get to that happy place. There was a time in my life when the words and the slurs used against me did hurt. That hurt eventually turned to anger, and the anger, in time, developed into my current attitude, which is simply, "I am who I am, so like it or lump it." It isn't always easy to find the positive in a negative or even traumatic situation, but taking a step back and asking oneself, "What did I learn from that?" can lead to one's becoming stronger and finding a way to stand tall in one's own shoes.

TESTING THE WATERS

Life can be difficult for kids who are trying to fit in—for whom fitting in can, in fact, be the difference between a happy childhood and a life of torment. We've all seen how devastating bullying can be for a child who is on the receiving end of such mean-spirited behavior. When those kids reach a breaking point they can either turn their anger outward and create a tragedy like the Columbine massacre or they can turn it inward and harm themselves. In fact, several of the kids I've worked with have stated that they just want "it" to be over, and if they didn't get help they were ready to kill themselves—not only because they were being teased or bullied by their peers but also because they didn't understand and couldn't control what they were receiving from the world of spirit. It takes a lot of support and understanding on the part of the adults in these kids' lives for them to survive it and ultimately thrive.

Most often the victims of bullying are those who are perceived to be different in some way, and being psychic, as I've said, is just another way of being different. Growing up, and even into adulthood, I've experienced more than my share of bullying (and not necessarily because I am psychic), and I certainly know what that feels like. What psychic kids who may find themselves becoming the butt of bullies need to understand is that sometimes, as the Bard said, "the better part of valor is discretion." There's a difference between being brave and being foolhardy. You wouldn't, for example, want to jump into uncharted waters without first making sure that they weren't infested with sharks.

Therefore, while it is, as I've said, important for psychic kids to have a safe person with whom they can discuss their experiences, it's equally important for them to know that they need to be discerning about how and to whom they talk about their psychic gift. It's probably not a good idea, for example, to give their peers unsolicited advice based upon precognitive information. In other words, don't flaunt it, and don't use your abilities to gain power over others. No one likes a show-off, and learning not to boast about your paranormal experiences isn't very different from what all kids should be learning about the dangers of bragging and/or manipulating others. But for psychic kids in particular there is the danger that talking too freely about their abilities could lead to their being ostracized.

One way to test the waters might be for the child to ask a friend in a general way what he or she thinks about psychic phenomena. The child might broach the subject by asking whether the friend has watched *Psychic Kids* and, if so, whether he believes those children really had psychic abilities. Or he could use another TV program, such as *Medium* or *Ghost Hunters*, as the point of discussion. Then, if the friend seemed open to the existence of these phenomena, he could bring up his own abilities. On the other hand, if the friend didn't seem open, he'd be able to figure that out before putting himself at risk.

But skepticism and nastiness aren't the prerogatives only of kids. Adults can be just as skeptical and even more hurtful. Therefore, kids need to know how to deal with teachers, doctors, counselors, and other adults who may be just as vicious, if not more so, than their peers. (The following chapter will deal entirely with the question of religious bigotry and why psychic abilities do not undermine or contradict anyone's personal religious beliefs.) And sometimes a child may need to turn to a trusted adult to step in and let it be known in no uncertain terms that he or she will not allow the child to be bullied or harassed by adults any more than by his peers.

SUICIDE IS *NEVER* THE ANSWER!

Young people attempt suicide at an alarmingly high rate. They can become emotionally distraught rather easily and thus are vulnerable to suicidal thoughts.

Here are some very troubling statistics:

- Suicide is the sixth leading cause of death among children ages five to fourteen.
- Suicide is the third leading cause of death among youths ages fifteen to twenty-four.
- A youth suicide (ages fifteen to twenty-four) occurs every one hundred minutes.

There are many reasons a young person may consider or attempt suicide:

- Death of a parent.
- Divorce of parents.
- Feeling like a "pawn" that is being used between feuding, divorced parents.
- Joining a new family with a stepparent and stepsiblings.
- Breaking up with a boyfriend/girlfriend.
- Moving to a new community.
- Not feeling accepted by peers.
- Being ridiculed by classmates.
- Feeling misunderstood.
- Any experience perceived to be humiliating.
- Alcohol abuse.
- Drug abuse.
- Being bullied by classmates.

And for psychic kids, we can add:

- Feeling overwhelmed by the inability to understand and manage psychic abilities and paranormal experiences.

Although some people who take their own life do not exhibit any warning signs at all, here are some of the red flags parents need to watch out for:

- Appearing depressed or sad most of the time. (Untreated depression is the number one cause for suicide.)
- Talking or writing about death or suicide.
- Withdrawing from family and friends.
- Feeling hopeless.

- Feeling helpless.
- Feeling strong anger or rage.
- Feeling trapped, like there is no way out of a situation.
- Experiencing dramatic mood changes.
- Abusing drugs or alcohol.
- Exhibiting a change in personality.
- Acting impulsively.
- Losing interest in most activities.
- Experiencing a change in sleeping habits.
- Experiencing a change in eating habits.
- Performing poorly at work or in school.
- Giving away prized possessions.
- Writing a will.
- Feeling excessive guilt or shame.
- Acting recklessly.

Constant, open communication with your children is extremely important. Parents need to establish an environment that fosters open communication. And children need to know that they can speak up when there is a problem with which they need help.

BE CAREFUL BUT DON'T BE AFRAID

Despite all I've just said, I also want psychic kids to know that they must learn to step into their power, and I want parents to understand that being psychic is a gift, not a disease or a handicap.

Parents brag about their kids' grades or their musical or athletic abilities, but they're not likely to brag about their psychic talents. That's okay. Bragging, as I've said, isn't a very attractive quality in any case. But they also need to let their kids know that being psychic is not something about which they should be ashamed, much less frightened.

As adults, parents (or anyone else who is guiding or mentoring a psychic child) usually have a better sense of the climate in which they live and the degree of tolerance the child is likely to encounter outside the home. I like to say that if you live in an area where you know there are wolves and coyotes, you wouldn't want to leave raw meat on your doorstep. Therefore, one reason it's so important for a psychic kid to be able to confide in an understanding adult is so that the adult can use the benefit of his or her greater experience and wisdom to guide the child through what could very well be some troubled waters.

The bottom line for parents is always to consider what is going to best serve their child. Be aware. If the child is thriving, that's great. But if he's having trouble in school, if psychic experiences are having a negative effect on his ability to study and concentrate, a parent may have to step in, go to the school authorities, and take a stand on behalf of his child. Can I guarantee that the so-called authorities will be open-minded and sympathetic to the problem? No, I can't. But sometimes being tough, taking on the role of Mama or Papa Bear in order to protect your cub by standing firm in the face of ignorance, is what you need to do. School is supposed to be a safe haven for kids, and if it isn't serving as that for your kid, you need to demand your rights (and the rights of your child) in no uncertain terms. I've even told parents that if the school system is telling them that their child is mentally unhealthy, they need to say, "Well then, you're telling me that my child has a handicap and if you don't protect him, I'm going to sue you for the way you're treating my handicapped child." I know that's extreme, but sometimes extreme situations demand extreme measures. If your child is being targeted or harassed, it's your obligation to be sure the school authorities know what's going on, know that *you* know what's going on, and know that you *will not* allow it to continue. One problem is that our public school system has remedies and protocols in place for children with all kinds of special needs, but because psychic kids are only now beginning to go public (or come out, so to speak), there is no plan in place for taking care of their special needs.

We've talked about how important a sense of community is for psychic kids who might otherwise feel isolated and alone, and I personally believe that the same holds true for their parents. Because there are no protocols in place, parents may be confused about what to do or feel they have nowhere to turn. Finding and communicating with others in their situation can, therefore, be as important for them as it is for their kids. Maybe this book will serve to create an opening for that kind of communication. My hope is that eventually there may even be support groups for the parents of psychic kids as there are for the parents of children with other kinds of challenges.

Some kids—teens in particular—may initially try to talk their parents out of interfering, either because they're embarrassed or because they're afraid it might just make things worse. Don't back down. There was never a television program called *Children Know Best*, because they don't—even when they think they do. What parents need to do then is assure their child that they understand his feelings, but, at the same time, let him know that whatever is going on isn't going to go away and will probably get worse if they *don't* intervene.

I believe that despite what they may say, beneath the bluster and protesting, kids want and need their parents to protect them.

YOU DON'T HAVE TO BROADCAST IT BUT YOU DO NEED TO OWN IT

I've certainly encountered more negativity since going public with my psychic abilities than I did while I was growing up, and I know that some of the families who appeared on *Psychic Kids* had some degree of backlash to deal with in the aftermath. In fact, we advised them in advance of their agreeing to do the show that this was likely to happen. While I commend the courage they showed in allowing us to broadcast their stories, I also understand that not everyone is willing or prepared to do that. That's okay, too. I certainly don't believe that it's wise to openly, or even potentially, invite negativity into your life. But I do believe that it's up to the responsible adults in every psychic child's life to help him understand how much and with whom to share what he's experiencing while also making it abundantly clear that he has nothing to be ashamed or afraid of. First and foremost, kids need to know that having paranormal experiences is not—and should not be—a "dirty little secret."

Beyond that, if a child does confide in his parents that he's being bullied, made fun of, or worse, how the parents react will certainly have an effect, positive or negative, on how the child reacts. This isn't really very different from what happens when any child is apprehensive or frightened and goes running to Mommy or Daddy for comfort. It's always the parent's role to remain calm and acknowledge and validate the child's fear, but also assure him that as a parent he or she will protect him and make sure he isn't harmed.

Learning not to be frightened of what other people might think is hard for a child, especially for a teenager, but it's never too early to plant the seed of self-confidence in the face of so much ignorance. There's a fine line between discretion and fear. Certainly there's no point in inviting ridicule or even physical harm by running around and announcing to everyone you meet, "Hey, I'm psychic." As my cousin Kenny so sagely says about no-win situations, "No good can come of this."

The problem is that skeptics are, for the most part, not really skeptics. The dictionary definition of a skeptic is "one who questions the validity or authenticity of something purporting to be factual; a person who maintains a doubting attitude." Healthy skepticism invites the demonstration of an opposing point of view. It also involves the willingness to keep an open mind about something that can't be proved or disproved (at least at this point in time). For example, people are constantly asking me about aliens, and my answer is that I don't yet know enough to have formed a definitive opinion, but I'm certainly open to the possibility that there are other life-forms in the universe.

I believe it takes a good deal of courage and intelligence to say "I don't know." That's a brave stance. But most skeptics I've met don't doubt or question; they don't require additional knowledge in order to form an opinion because they already *know* that they are right and you are wrong. That's not a skeptic; it's a 100 percent disbeliever. And because of that, these people can be extremely hostile and aggressive in their response to anyone who believes in or has had experiences of the paranormal. They tend to harass, ridicule, and berate anyone whose belief system is different from their own. There's nothing open to debate;

there's nothing open to discussion. Therefore, trying to convince them is about as useful as rearranging the deck chairs on the *Titanic*. Moving the furniture wouldn't prevent the ship from sinking, and arguing with a disbeliever is nothing more than a frustrating exercise in futility.

These people will always be out there, and once a child lets it be known (either publicly, as the kids who appeared on our program did, or by talking about it with friends) that he's had psychic or paranormal experiences, those so-called skeptics will be bound and determined to bombard him with their opinions. There's really no way to prevent that, and the best advice I can give parents about how to help their kid withstand the fallout is first to make it clear that there may be repercussions and then simply to do whatever they can to insulate him from any negativity. Advise him not to read or leave comments on message boards, not to look himself up on the Internet, and, in general, to do what he can to avoid getting jabbed by the barbs that are almost certain to be coming his way. To the degree that it's possible, the only way to deal with disbelievers is to turn a blind eye and a deaf ear. They don't want to hear anything that anyone else might have to say and any attempt at self-defense is only going to throw fuel on the fire.

When I first started to appear in public and on television I was constantly checking the Internet to see what people were saying about me, and sometimes their comments were incredibly nasty and hurtful. The best advice anyone ever gave me was not to read those comments and never to respond. Skeptics love a good fight, and by responding all I'd be doing is letting them know that they succeeded in both hurting and engaging me.

So, while I certainly don't encourage kids to flaunt their abilities indiscreetly, I also don't want them to let other people's ignorance erode their confidence. I don't want them to live in fear of what others might think or allow another person to define them.

Getting there has been a struggle for me. Even now the comments of strangers sometimes get to me, and when that happens I just have to step back and remind myself that these people don't know me and if I let them get under my skin, the only one being hurt is going to be me. I'll be handing over my power and they will win. I no longer allow that to happen. Much of that kind of empowerment and confidence, however, simply comes with age and maturity.

CHECKLIST FOR PARENTS

- Explain that there will always be doubters and naysayers in the world.
- Teach your child when to be discreet and when to share.
- Help him to learn how to "test the waters."
- Help your kid step into his power and not let anyone else define who he is or should be.

CHAPTER SIX

God Never Had Anything Against Psychics

B rad S. comes from a very fundamentalist religious family, and the fact that he is a psychic medium had created an enormous rift between him and his parents. Brad's mother and father know now that his psychic ability is a God-given gift he is able to use for the purpose of doing good in the world. Initially, however, that was far from the way they viewed it. When we met on *Psychic Kids*, Brad was a sweet-faced and equally sweet-tempered eighteen-year-old who exhibited a high level of psychic ability, but his mother, Missy, believed that Brad's abilities were "not of God" and that what he needed to do was to "get rid of them." As she saw it there was "an opposing force" (i.e., the devil) that wanted him "on their side." Not surprisingly, Brad had become extremely alienated from his family, and, from his mom's point of view, he was shunning his parents. He, for his part, felt that he was disappointing his parents and only wanted them to understand that his gift was a part of him—not something being imposed upon him by the devil—and that he could use it for good, not evil.

From the beginning I knew that resolving the rift between Brad and his family would be difficult, if not impossible, but I also believed it was extremely important to bring about some kind of understanding and reconciliation between Brad and his parents. Those of us involved with the program decided that one way to show his parents how a psychic gift can be used for good was to get Brad and Santana, the teenage girl with him on the retreat, involved in some psychic detective work. The case involved a nineteen-year-old girl who had vanished two years before and whose disappearance had never been resolved. After the kids met with the girl's mother and Tom Shamshak, the private detective working the cold case, we took them to the house where the girl had been living when she went missing. Their ability to pick up psychic information and provide new leads to the investigator, combined with the profound gratitude expressed by the girl's mother (who didn't seem to find them weird at all and later told their parents they were "wonderful kids"), finally brought Brad's mother around to seeing things differently.

First of all, she admitted that "he needs to become what God wants him to become." She was relieved to find that no one had tried to, as she put it, "take [her] God away from" her during our time to-gether. And, in the end, she said, "I think I'm seeing that he's found something that he's good at and I was seeing it the wrong way." The climactic moment came when she was able to say, "I love you," to her son. They hugged, and she said, "You haven't hugged me in a real long time." It was a miraculous moment, and I assure you that there wasn't a dry eye in the house. After that, Brad's mother was able to get his dad on board as well and to tell her son, "We're totally behind you."

TOM SHAMSHAK TALKS ABOUT PSYCHIC INVESTIGATION

I've worked with Tom Shamshak on several occasions and have always been both impressed and gratified by his openness to paranormal experiences. Tom's career as a law enforce-ment professional began in 1978 when he joined the police department in Somerville, Massachusetts, ultimately rising to the rank of lieutenant and directing the Somerville Police Academy. In 1990 he left Somerville to become police chief for the town of Spencer in central Massachusetts. And from there he moved on to Winthrop, Massachusetts, where he was chief until retiring in 1999 and opening his own private investigation firm.

Tom's first experience of collaborating with a psychic occurred in 2006 when he received a phone call from close friends whose daughter had gone missing (and was subse-quently found to be a murder victim). Telling him that they'd received a call from the producers of the television program

Haunting Evidence, who said they would like to do an episode about their daughter's case, Tom's friends wanted to know whether he thought they should agree. Tom, who admits to approaching the idea of psychic forensic abilities with "a healthy dose of skepticism," nevertheless said, "Hey, leave no stone unturned," and later, when offered the opportunity, he also participated in the episode.

"I was very impressed by the information that the psychics were able to come up with in relation to the unsolved murder," Tom said.

After that experience, he appeared on four episodes of *Psychic Kids* and came to one of my Coffey Talks in Boston, where he also met with several local psychics and ultimately founded a group called the Cold Case Collaborative that brings psychics together at Boston University, where Tom is director and lead instructor of the certificate program in professional investigation. The group's objective is to try to figure out exactly how psychic abilities can best be utilized in conjunction with traditional police procedures in order to solve crimes. One of the youngsters Tom worked with on *Psychic Kids* was Brad S., who is now a member of the collaborative.

When I asked Tom why—given his professional background in traditional law enforcement—he was so open to using psychic investigators, he told me the following.

Based on my participation in *Psychic Kids*, my curiosity was piqued. I was very impressed by these teenagers, and I'm trying to understand more about their unique abilities. I'm open to thinking outside the box. Using a psychic is another invaluable tool. I firmly believe that intuitive individuals have an innate ability to look at the world a little differently, and that's what I'm trying to explore. I believe that any investigator worth his or her salt should explore the use of a psychic or medium as part of the investigative tool box.

I've learned, particularly from my appearances on *Psychic Kids*, that these kids can at least corroborate and support my own intuitive thinking. They've been accurate enough in identifying certain aspects of the case—a tattoo or a piercing—that I'm satisfied they're able to focus in on this information. How do we enhance and explore that tool? Maybe using technology in the field—listening for voices. How can we get that spirit to lead us to physical evidence?

When I'm working with a psychic, there are three things I look for: Can you give me an individual? Can you direct me to a place with some specificity? Can you identify an object? I could be looking for a missing person or looking for a person or persons around that person who might be responsible for his or her death. Is there a body? Where is the body? Where might physical evidence be? What caused the death? Was there a weapon? What weapon? Police investigators look for physical evidence (a body), documentary evidence (such as telephone records, a diary), and testimonial evidence (interviewing people who might have information). What I'd like to be able to do is infuse these standard investigative techniques with the psychic component.

One of the exercises I did with the group at Boston University was to show them photographs of missing people from cases I'd been involved with and whose outcomes I already knew. I'd give a group of psychics a photo and a description of the person. They'd sit there for a few minutes jotting down notes and then let me know that they had a "bad" feeling about someone or that another person seemed to be "okay." What I found is that they were extremely accurate about "feeling" which of these people were dead and which ones had been found alive and well.

What I would like to do is create a paradigm or procedure through which psychic information can be infused into contemporary investigative methodology. The technology has changed. We have GPS for normal people. Why can't we learn to harness this psychic energy so that it can bring us home?

Who am I not to use any potential resource that might be available to me?

"PSYCHIC" IS NOT A SYNONYM FOR "SATANIC"

When I was about six weeks old, it became necessary for me to undergo a risky surgical procedure. My parents were told that my chance of survival was only about 30 percent. Immediately after receiving this devastating news, my mother walked from the hospital to a church across the street, where she began to pray, "God, please don't take my child away from me. I don't think that I could bear to lose another child. I promise that if You allow my child to live, I will encourage him to do Your work." My mother's prayers were answered, and throughout the remainder of her life, she did encourage me to remain faithful to God. I truly believe that the work I am doing as a psychic, medium, and spiritual counselor is God's work. I am honored to be able to fulfill the promise my mother made to God on that October day back in 1954.

But not everyone sees it that way. As an adult, I have been accused more than once of consorting with the devil and even threatened with excommunication from the Catholic Church. I choose not to engage in discussion or debate with those who seek to use theology or their religious beliefs as a weapon against me because, in most instances, trying to reason or argue with a religious zealot is nothing more than an exercise in futility. But for many psychic kids growing up in a religious family and/or community, trying to maintain that kind of composure can be at best difficult and at worst devastating. It's not only parents who are willing to disown their own kids if they believe they are doing the work of the devil. I've also known religious leaders who condemn psychic children from the pulpit as disciples of Satan. These children are not tainted, they are not damaged, and above all, they are not instruments of the devil.

You'd think that religious leaders would be *more* accepting than the less enlightened members of their flock, but very often it is those very leaders who are the most closed minded. Nick, whom we met in chapter 4, was publicly condemned in the newspaper by a local minister after the program aired and his encounters with Mr. Rosenberg were made public. Personally, while writing this book I reached out to one particular priest for an opinion on paranormal phenomena only to have him tell me in no uncertain terms that he wanted nothing at all to do with me or my book (and I wasn't asking him to agree with me, only to give an opinion).

Happily, however, there are other members of the clergy who are open to the existence of paranormal experiences. Probably the best-known of them is Father Bob Bailey of Saint Maria Goretti Parish in Pawtucket, Rhode Island, who, with the full cooperation of his bishop, participated in several episodes of the television programs *Paranormal State* and *The Haunted* and has become very involved in the investigation of paranormal activities. When I met Father Bob I was very pleased to hear him say, "I am very open to people with psychic abilities because I believe that those abilities are a gift from God."

In light of the ridicule, not to mention potential persecution, they invite by their open-mindedness, Father Bob and others like him are, I believe, to be commended as brave warriors against bigotry, ignorance, and fear.

While there's nothing I—or anyone else—can do to change the minds of bigots, religious or otherwise, I do entreat everyone to understand that each one of us is entitled to his or her own beliefs, free from ridicule or persecution by those who do not believe the same.

Once in a meditative moment I asked the universe, "What is the meaning of life?" The answer I received was, "Chip, the meaning of life is simple. Just get through it the best way you can." Well, I thought that was a bit glib, so I said, "Hey, wait a minute. Could you just extrapolate on that a bit?" And the answer I got then was, "All the universe, or God, or your spirit guides want from you is to do no intentional harm to yourself or others and to get happy!" The more I thought about that, the more sense it made. It has now become the mantra by which I live my life.

I believe that we are all put on this earth to learn lessons and fulfill our soul's destiny. And if we don't learn those lessons the first time, we keep coming back until we do. Our soul, in its purest form, wants to be as close to God, or divine perfection, as possible. That's the reason we try to better ourselves. And nothing about doing that contradicts what any religion teaches. In fact, all religions teach us to get as close to God as we can and to be as good a person as we can be in whatever way we can. In John 3:7 Jesus says, "You must be born again," which is generally taken to mean that one must be baptized and/or rededicate oneself to Christianity, but what if Jesus is actually saying that, if you want to get as close as possible to His Father, you have to keep being reborn until you get it right? What if He is talking about reincarnation?

I believe that my ability is a gift from God, and at the end of every day I give thanks for the gift I've been given. I cherish it, and I use it to bring healing to others. I tell the children I work with—as I urge all parents to tell their psychic children—"You are a child of God. God made you. If God didn't want you to have these abilities, He wouldn't have given them to you."

GOD MADE US ALL

God made every one of us, and we then created religion. Since then men (and religious leaders of all denominations are still mostly men) have been using the name of God to condemn anyone who dares to question their particular religion. And people of all denominations have been forced to capitulate, recant, deny their beliefs, or suffer religious persecution.

America was founded by people who fled their home country to seek religious freedom, but religious bigotry is still alive and kicking in many segments of American society today. Basically, what religious bigots are saying is, "I will tell you what to believe and if you don't get with the program you will be excommunicated and shunned." But if you truly believe that God created all men and that He is all-powerful, how can you then not believe that He loves all of us equally?

And to those who quote scripture in the service of their own narrow-minded beliefs I would quote from Matthew 7:1, "Judge not, that ye be not judged." But if you quote from the Bible to support your own beliefs (or prejudices), it is almost certain that that there will be another passage to support an opposing belief. Anyone can find a biblical passage to suit his own purpose, but you don't get to be what I call an à la carte believer. You don't get to pick and choose which passages are to your taste and which ones are not. If there are some biblical shalts and shalt-nots that we clearly recognize as being outmoded, how can we then state that some others are not—just because we happen to agree with some and disagree with others? How can any individual profess to know better than others what is or is not in the heart and mind of God?

WHAT IT MEANS TO HAVE FAITH

Saint Augustine states in one of his sermons that "faith is to believe what you do not see." So why is it that those who have faith in God or a Higher Power who cannot be seen and whose existence cannot be proved are so often the very ones who are quickest to condemn other people's faith in the existence of a spirit world and the ability to communicate with those in spirit? Why should anyone else get to decide whose belief system is acceptable and whose is not?

In fact, it seems to me that people who have faith in the existence of a Higher Power should be those most likely to be open-minded about paranormal experiences. And, conversely, it would seem more logical that those who deny the existence of God would also be the ones most likely to deny the existence of a spirit world. When it comes to religious bigotry, however, logic has nothing to do with it.

NOTE TO PARENTS

Please do not allow your religious beliefs to come between you and your psychic child. Do not allow the beliefs of others to come between you and your child. If you believe in God, do you not also believe in an afterlife? And if you believe there is a life after death, can you not also believe in our ability to communicate with those in the world of spirit?

I consider my own relationship with God to be extremely personal and profound, and yours should be too. I would never ask anyone to give up or even question his or her own faith. My goal is to open minds, not to close them. All I ask is that people open their minds and hearts to the possibility that there is something going on in the universe that cannot (yet) be proved. That, to me, is true faith.

To call upon God as an instrument of hate rather than an instrument of love is the definition of what it means to take the name of the Lord in vain.

CHAPTER SEVEN

Moving into Adulthood

With maturity, experience, and personal growth, I've gotten to the point, as I've said, where I don't pay too much attention to other people's opinion of me; I don't let other people's negativity define who I am. I have simply tried to use my abilities to create a career and earn a living, and while I'm doing that, to have some positive influence on the world and on the lives of others.

It hasn't always been easy and I've certainly taken my share of knocks along the way, but most of those have come from people who really don't know me. I consider myself lucky that while I was growing up I was never made to feel I was in any way "not normal." I certainly realized at some point that not everyone received precognitive information as I did (at that point I still didn't know that I was also a medium), but anyone who knew about my abilities was always extremely supportive of me. My mother, based on her own psychic abilities and out-of-body, near-death experience at the time of my birth, never doubted the existence of paranormal events. And her friend Jane Norwood had a positive influence on me as an adolescent boy. My mother met Jane at about the time we moved into the haunted house in Elmira. Jane was very intuitive and did card readings using a standard deck of playing cards rather than a tarot deck. She'd somehow come up with a particular meaning for each card and had written the meanings on the cards in her beat-up old deck. She was also a self-taught graphologist who could look at people's handwriting and intuitively determine things about them from their writing. Because of her own abilities, she made me feel "normal," and although she wasn't a teacher to me, she did serve as a role model and let me know that I was okay.

Another of my mother's friends, Betty Kane, was also very interested in metaphysical and spiritual phenomena. Sadly, the death of her husband, Tom, was also the occasion for one of my most unusual paranormal experiences. There was a legend in my family that when someone close to the family died, a family member would see a white dove inside the house flying from one corner of the room to another. I'd heard the story growing up but had never witnessed it myself. I had graduated college and was living with my family in Sarasota, Florida, where Betty and her husband also lived. Tom had been diagnosed with multiple myeloma and was in the hospital near death. I was working for the Head Start program and was on summer vacation at the time. I remember sitting in the living room watching television when I looked up and saw a white bird fly diagonally across the living room and disappear. Within moments, the phone rang. It was my mother, who had been at the hospital with Betty. "Chip," she said, "I have something I've got to tell you." And I said, "I know, Tom is dead." When she asked how I could possibly have known that, I told her about seeing the bird. Although I'd never seen it before, I was aware of the family legend and recognized what was happening when the bird appeared.

After her husband died, Betty enrolled in a metaphysical school in Sarasota. I went to a couple of classes with her, and she subsequently helped to expand my consciousness and encouraged me to accept that nothing is completely beyond the realm of possibility.

For whatever reason, people who were interested in various aspects of spirituality and paranormal phenomena seemed to be drawn to my family. We didn't talk about it very much, and aside from the fact that a few of my relatives wanted me to do card readings for them and their friends, it never occurred to me that my abilities were a big deal. My parents also protected me by letting me know that not everyone would be receptive to the experiences I was having or to the collective experiences of the family. They helped me to understand that it might not be prudent of me to talk too freely about our having lived in a haunted house or about the precognitive messages I received. My father's attitude was that this was personal family business that needed to be kept within the family. And neither of my parents wanted me to become anyone's "pet psychic" or have my gift used to perform psychic circus tricks for my friends.

It ought to be the primary goal of any parent, teacher, or counselor (or any adult, for that matter) to love and nurture the children with whom she comes in contact in a way that prepares them to go out into the world as strong, resilient, kind, and compassionate adults. In other words, it is our job as adults to prepare children—psychic or otherwise—to launch.

My hope is that, with the information I've provided, all members of every community will be better able to do that for the psychic children who come into their lives.

At some point psychic kids have to determine whether using their abilities will become their career path. For me that took many years, but I now realize that my life up to the point where I decided to "go public" and become a professional psychic had been giving me the foundation and life skills I needed to succeed. Becoming a child actor and model (my first modeling job was posing for a calendar when I was exactly two years, two months, and two days old) taught me to be comfortable before an audience and a camera. I was performing throughout elementary school, high school, and on into college. I grew comfortable getting up in front of people to speak, and I also learned my way around television and movie sets. Studying psychology and counseling (particularly child and adolescent psychology and family therapy) taught me to understand the human psyche. For a decade I was a successful producer of children's theater in Atlanta, which taught me how to work well with children. Finally, being in the travel industry allowed me to become comfortable as a frequent traveler and learn how to settle in quickly in a new and unfamiliar location.

Since becoming a full-time psychic, medium, and spiritual counselor in 2001, I have conducted thousands of readings for clients all around the world, including television and film stars, professional athletes, politicians, and business moguls. For me, being a professional psychic was not an initial career choice, but it has been an extremely rewarding one. Being able to help and guide people so that they feel better about themselves and move on to leading more positive and productive lives has been tremendously fulfilling for me.

When I do public appearances, I am often asked to share stories about interesting readings I have done, and one that continues to fascinate my audiences occurred soon after I began offering readings to the general public. A woman named Vicki called me because she was hoping to reconnect with her significant other, Tom. I immediately felt that Tom had died unexpectedly of a massive heart attack, and Vicki confirmed that this was true. Tom had been installing a hot tub on the deck of their home, began to feel ill, collapsed in their dining room, and died in Vicki's arms.

Spirits whom I contact during "crossing over"–type readings almost always come through displaying personalities that are very similar to the ones they had while residing in the living world. Tom's energy came booming through to me, and I knew that when alive, he had been an outgoing and gregarious man.

He was quick-witted, with a bawdy sense of humor. In fact, I remember telling Vicki that he was a bit of a smart aleck because he kept calling me "Whoopi," referring to Whoopi Goldberg's psychic and medium character in the hit movie *Ghost*. During the reading, he provided Vicki with precise details about their lives together, and knowing that Tom carried memories of the times they shared together into the afterlife gave Vicki great comfort.

Oftentimes, reconnecting with deceased loved ones is a very emotional experience and many tears are shed, but sometimes there are also humorous moments, and Tom provided one of those moments; he told me, "Tell Vicki I like the way her ass looks in her new jeans." When I relayed this message, she laughed heartily and said, "Yep, that's my Tom! I just bought a new pair of jeans a few days ago and I'm wearing them for the first time. That's exactly what he would have said when he saw me in them!"

I love to share my stories and have included a few more of my favorites in appendix B of this book. But while going pro has many rewards, there are undeniably also some drawbacks. Once you become a public figure in any field of endeavor, you are opening your private life to public scrutiny. And if your area of expertise is paranormal phenomena, you are also opening yourself up to doubters and haters who feel completely free to ridicule and deride what you do even though they don't understand it. Some people may not want to expose themselves in this way, and it's certainly something psychic kids need to understand and take into account as they move into adulthood and decide whether or not to become professional psychics. For me, however, the rewards have far outweighed the problems, and the people who respect and admire what I do far outnumber those who seek to discredit me.

Even if a psychic child decides not to turn pro, however, she can (and I believe should) continue to use her abilities for the greater good and, whenever possible, to help other people. Without trespassing on another person's privacy, and without thrusting information on people without asking their permission, those of us who have psychic gifts also have the opportunity to guide and lead in a way others may not. To do that, we just need to keep our spiritual eyes and ears open, so that we recognize those opportunities when they arise.

Those who believe in a spiritual realm beyond the earthly plane also subscribe to the existence of a mystical compendium of knowledge known as the Akashic records, which contain all the knowledge in the universe. We are all a part of this universal plan and are put on earth with a script to follow, even though we may not recognize it as such and our own free will may lead us to digress from the script or fail to recognize our role in the "play" as a whole.

When we're following the script and things are going well, we may experience what someone once described to me as "God winks" and what I call divine synchronicity. We may think of these instances as fortuitous coincidences or "wow moments," but they are actually circumstances that were meant to be—part of the divine plan. They are God's way of reminding us that He is with us, that we have everything we need to create our best life. All we have to do is figure out how to use what we've been given. I think of our soul plan as a giant jigsaw puzzle. All the pieces are in the box, but we need to put the pieces together. We are co-creators with the universe; opportunities will be presented to us, but when they are, we need to recognize what's coming at us and make the most of what we are given. In the football game of life God would be the quarterback throwing us a pass. We need to be alert enough not only to catch the ball but also to take it over the line and score a touchdown.

People are put in our path at a particular time because they have a lesson to teach us or because we have one to teach them. We are always in the right place at the right time. Recognizing those moments and acting upon them is the way—as the universe put it to me—to get through life the best way you can. Each lesson we learn contributes to our soul's growth, allows us to move up a grade in the school of the soul, and takes us one step closer to the ultimate goal of becoming as close to divine perfection as we can. Our spirit guides are those who have evolved to a higher level of soul knowledge and who, therefore, are able to act as teachers and mentors to those of us who haven't yet arrived at their level of illumination. By learning these soul lessons, kids who are growing up psychic, like all the rest of us, will be doing what is necessary in order to become the best adults they can be.

Epilogue

Here I am, teetering on the brink of being labeled a senior citizen, but I'm still a "psychic kid" at heart.

My life has been filled with many great experiences. Sometimes the road has been a bit bumpy, but everything in my past has led me to the present and will guide me toward the future. As philosopher Friedrich Nietzsche said, "That which does not kill us makes us stronger." And as Sir Elton John so aptly sang, "I'm still standing better than I ever did . . ."

I take nothing for granted because I know that it could all be over in the blink of an eye.

Regrets? Honestly, not many. We cannot rewrite the past, nor can we "unring a bell," so I refuse to be a victim of regrets. I don't trouble myself with a lot of "shoulda, woulda, coulda."

I've heard some psychics refer to their abilities as a "curse," but, as I've said, I consider my abilities to be an immense and joyful blessing, and that is why I've learned to embrace and manage them. I would never reject or regret my psychic abilities because that, to me, would be akin to spitting in the eye of God.

Unashamedly, I am a man of strong faith. I have a firm, unwavering belief in God. (That's the term I use to refer to my Higher Power, but feel free to choose your own.) I pray to God many times every day and thank Him for allowing me to do His work. I've got the greatest "boss" in the entire universe!

There are many things that I hope to do before I make my own transition back into the world of spirit. What's on my "bucket list"? I intend to continue my career as a psychic and medium, helping others to the best of my abilities. I love to travel, to visit new places and meet new people. One of my goals is to visit all fifty of the United States; as of this writing, I've visited forty-six. I also hope to travel more in Europe. I spent eight days in France many years ago, but I'd like to return and also see England and Ireland while I'm "across the pond." I plan to continue my efforts with animal rescue, and I'll never stop speaking out *loudly* against prejudice, abuse, and bullying.

On the TV show *Inside the Actors Studio*, host James Lipton always asks his guests a list of ten interview questions, based on a questionnaire created by Bernard Pivot, a French television personality. The final question is this: "If heaven exists, what would you like to hear God say when you arrive at the pearly gates?"

This is my answer: "Welcome home, Chip. You did good."

Growing up psychic has certainly been quite an adventure. I survived and I thrived . . . and others like me can, too!

GLOSSARY

Following are some of the more common terms you may find in this book and in other sources dealing with paranormal activities.

afterlife: the state of being after the death of the physical body.

Akashic records: a term used to describe a total collection of mystical knowledge that is "housed" in a nonphysical plane; the Akashic records are often metaphorically described as a library, computer, or "the mind of God" and are said to contain a complete account of everything (thought and action) that has occurred, is occurring, or will occur in the entire universe.

angels: divine beings that act as intermediaries between heaven and earth; God's helpers; beings created by God to serve as His emissaries. Angels typically do not incarnate into human form for a full lifetime, but will sometimes take human shape in order to assist the living. From my own perspective, the souls of the living do not "transform into" angels after death.

apparition: the supernatural manifestation of a person, animal, or thing in physical form. Apparitions may take the form of a life-like full body, or they may be hazy or shadowy, or appear as a partial body.

apportation: the paranormal transference of an article from one place to another, or the appearance of an article from an unknown source, often associated with poltergeist activity and spiritualistic séances. (*See also* asportation, teleportation)

asportation: the disappearance of an object that reappears elsewhere or not at all. (*See also* apportation, teleportation)

astral projection or astral travel: the intentional act of the spirit (or soul or consciousness) to leave the physical body. (*See also* near-death experience, out-of-body experience)

aura: energy that emanates from and surrounds all living things. Some individuals profess to have the ability to see these energy fields. The color(s) of a person's aura is said to indicate his or her mental, emotional, or physical state at the time.

automatic writing: the act of communicating with disincarnate beings by allowing their energy to guide one's hand when writing. Typically, an individual will sit with pen (or other writing instrument) in hand, clear his mind (or make a conscious attempt to communicate), and allow the spirit energy to move his hand, thus creating a written message.

chakra: term originating in Hindu texts referring to each of the seven energy centers that are located at various points throughout both the physical and "spiritual" bodies: at the crown (located at the top of or slightly above the head); in the middle of the forehead (between the eyebrows); at the throat, heart, solar plexus (between the chest and abdomen), and lower abdomen; and in the genital area. Chakras are often depicted as wheels and, sometimes, a lotus flower. The function of the chakras is to spin and draw in universal life-force energy to keep the spiritual, mental, emotional, and physical health of the body in balance.

channeling: the act of communicating with disincarnate beings.

chi: (pronounced *chee*) Chinese word meaning natural energy of the universe; a life force that is present in every living thing.

clairalient: (French, loosely translated as "clear smelling") possessing a form of extrasensory perception that gives one the ability to smell things beyond the normal. Also, a person who claims to possess this ability.

clairaudient: (French, loosely translated as "clear hearing") possessing a form of extrasensory perception that gives one the ability to hear things beyond normal hearing. Also, a person who claims to possess this ability.

clairsentient: (French, loosely translated as "clear sensing") possessing a form of extrasensory perception that gives one the ability to sense information and energy that cannot be perceived by the five natural senses. Also, a person who claims to possess this ability.

clairvoyant: (French, loosely translated as "clear seeing") possessing a form of extrasensory perception that gives one the ability to perceive future events or access information that cannot be perceived by the five natural senses; a form of extrasensory perception. Also, a person who claims to possess this ability.

cold spot: a location at which the temperature is lower than the surrounding environment. Many believe that the presence of ghosts or spirits may affect temperature, usually making an area colder, or less often, hotter.

crystal children: *See* indigo children

crystals: any of a wide variety of stones and gems that purportedly have energetic and/or healing properties.

curse: an appeal or prayer for evil or misfortune to befall someone or something. There are many varying beliefs and opinions about whether or not curses work and why they work. (Frequent synonym: "evil spell")

déjà vu: (French for "already seen") the phenomenon of feeling as though something similar (or identical) to what is happening in the present has occurred in the past. Some believe that déjà vu is indicative of past-life memories. Others believe that prior to incarnating into human form our souls plan or "write a script" for what will ideally occur during the upcoming lifetime and that déjà vu is the soul's brief and sporadic remembrance of the plan or script.

demon: an evil entity that is the devil's minion; a fallen angel. Demons blaspheme God and seek the ruin of souls by creating chaos among the living.

discernment: traditionally, "discernment" is defined as "the act or process of exhibiting keen insight and good judgment." Within the spiritual arena, the term "discernment" is often used to describe the ability to sense the difference between positive and negative supernatural energies. Some religions believe that discernment is "calling on God to lead or give direction on a matter."

disincarnate: disembodied; divested of the body. Ghosts and spirits are disincarnate beings. (Frequent synonym: "noncorporeal")

dissociative identity disorder (DID): a psychiatric disorder in which a person displays multiple, distinct personalities, known as alter egos or alters, each with its own unique personality traits. Formerly known as multiple personality disorder. Some psychic children have been misdiagnosed as suffering from DID.

divination: the art or act of foretelling future events or revealing occult knowledge. Often, various tools such as tarot cards, runes, *I Ching* wands or coins, or crystal balls may be used in the process of divination.

dybbuk: in Jewish folklore, a dybbuk is an evil spirit that may be malicious or malevolent. The term is also used to describe a parasitic entity that overtakes the body of a living being in order to experience or fulfill something that did not occur in its own lifetime. The dybbuk supposedly departs from its host body once its mission has been accomplished.

electromagnetic field (EMF): a physical field produced by electrically charged objects. Many paranormal researchers believe that disincarnate energies emit electrical energy that affects surrounding electromagnetic fields and/or absorb energy from available power sources in order to facilitate their crossing over into the living realm. During many paranormal investigations, EMF readings are taken with one or more of a variety of different instruments or meters. Some of the most popular EMF detectors include various Gauss meters, the K-2 meter, and numerous styles of Mel meters.

electronic voice phenomenon (EVP): unexplainable voices or other sounds that are captured on recording devices. Generally, these voices or sounds are not heard during the recording process but are present during playback. EVPs are generally graded by class according to their clarity: Class A is extremely clear and recognizable; Class B is somewhat clear and definable; Class C is generally unclear and unrecognizable, although it is evident that an unexplainable sound was recorded.

empath: a person who is very sensitive to the feelings, the emotions, and, often, the physical state of other beings. Empaths are also frequently affected by environmental energies at random locations. Many empaths must figure out methods to control their empathic abilities in order to prevent themselves from being constantly bombarded by emotions and energies.

exorcism: the process of expelling or attempting to expel an evil spirit or demon from a person, place, or thing. Formal exorcism is almost always performed by a member of the clergy, whereas "prayers of deliverance" may be said by either clergy or laypersons. Exorcisms may last for weeks, months, or even years. (*See also* possession)

extrasensory perception (ESP): the ability to receive information not through the recognized physical senses but with the mind. (Frequent synonyms: "psychic ability," "sixth sense")

free will: the ability to choose one's own life path, free from the constraints of luck, fate, destiny, and/or divine will.

fundamentalist religion: any religion that mandates strict, literal adherence to its principles and beliefs by its followers.

ghost: although the terms "ghost" and "spirit" are regularly used as synonyms, I believe the two entities are quite different from each other. Both ghosts and spirits are disincarnate energies, the essence or soul of a once-living being. Once that energy departs the body, generally at the time of death, the soul, which is still empowered with free will, may elect to remain on the earthly plane or continue onward into the spirit realm. Those who choose to stay "earthbound"—for various reasons, including fear of judgment by God or a Higher Power, unfinished business with the living, etc.—are energies I refer to as ghosts. Those who choose to move into the spirit realm (or afterlife or heaven) are energies I refer to as spirits.

haunted: a person, place, or thing may be haunted. Although usually associated with negative activity, the word "haunted" really means the presence of ghosts or spirits and the occurrence of paranormal activity.

holistic: emphasizing the importance of the whole and the interdependence of its parts. Holistic healing and its practitioners focus on the integration and wellness of body, mind, and spirit.

holy water: water that has been sanctified by a priest for the purpose of baptism and the blessing of persons, places, and objects, or, predominantly among Roman Catholics, as a means of repelling evil.

I Ching: an ancient Chinese text used in a form of divination that involves the tossing of six coins or wands. The resulting pattern (out of sixty-four possible outcomes) is then interpreted by reading its meaning in the text.

indigo children: the label given to certain children who supposedly possess special, unusual, and/or supernatural traits and abilities. Descriptions of indigo children include the belief that they are empathic, curious, strong-willed, independent, and often perceived by friends and family as being strange; that they possess a clear sense of self-definition and purpose; and that they exhibit a strong inclination toward spiritual matters from early childhood. Indigo children have also been described as having a strong feeling of entitlement or "deserving to be here." Personally, I prefer to use the more generic term "psychic children" or "psychic kids" when referring to youngsters with paranormal abilities. (Frequent synonyms: "crystal children," "star children")

intelligent haunting: the presence of disincarnate energies that seem to possess the ability to communicate with the living through various means, such as electronic voice phenomena, temperature changes, changes in electromagnetic fields, etc. Ghosts and spirits who interact with the living create intelligent hauntings. (*See also* residual haunting)

interdimensional transcommunication: communication between two distinct dimensions or realms (e.g., the realm of the living and the spirit realm).

intuitive: someone with a heightened sense of awareness and the ability to receive paranormal or supernatural information and messages. (Frequent synonyms: "psychic," "sensitive")

kabbalah (one of many various spellings): a body of mystical teachings of Jewish rabbinical origin, often based on an esoteric interpretation of the Hebrew scriptures.

karma: the concept that every action causes a particular reaction and that positive actions create positive reactions (and vice versa).

The effects may be seen immediately or be delayed. The delay can be until later in the present life or until the next. Most teachings say that for common mortals, being involved with karma is an unavoidable part of daily living.

matrixing: a psychological phenomenon involving a vague and random stimulus being perceived as significant. A common example of matrixing is seeing faces, animals, and other forms in clouds. Within the paranormal field, finding faces and shapes within indistinct, often shadowy forms is often, in fact, matrixing. The human brain naturally attempts to create order out of chaos; therefore, matrixing is a natural function of human cognitive processing. (Frequent synonym: "pareidolia")

meditation: an act or practice done in order to alter consciousness and realize some benefit. There are many forms of meditation, including controlled breathing, chanting, and body posturing. Some forms of meditation are related to particular religious traditions.

medium: an individual who has the ability to communicate with entities who reside in other realms or dimensions, including the realm of the dead. (Frequent synonyms: "spirit channel," "channeler")

meridians: in traditional Chinese medicine, meridians are pathways through which life-force energy is believed to flow.

metaphysics: the branch of philosophy that examines the ultimate nature of reality, existence, and experience.

mezuzah (one of many various spellings): a parchment inscribed with specific Bible passages and attached in a case to the doorpost of a Jewish house as a sign of faith. Some believe that a mezuzah will also protect against evil.

near-death experience (NDE): a phenomenon associated with a wide range of personal experiences recounted by individuals who have been revived after being pronounced clinically dead or those who have been very close to death. These experiences may include detachment from the body; feelings of levitation; extreme fear; total serenity, security, or warmth; the experience of absolute dissolution; the presence of a blinding light; various other sights and sounds; the sensation of traveling rapidly through a foggy tunnel; and, sometimes, reunions with deceased loved ones or contact with celestial or divine beings. The term "near-death experience" was coined by Dr. Raymond Moody, a medical doctor and parapsychologist, in his 1975 book *Life After Life*. (*See also* astral projection, out-of-body experience)

necromancy: a form of magic or divination that consists of summoning and communicating with the dead.

noncorporeal: *See* disincarnate

occult: relating to the paranormal, supernatural, mystical, or magical. "Occult" also means hidden from view or beyond the scope of human comprehension.

oppression: prolonged cruel or unjust treatment and control. In the spiritual or supernatural sense, oppression occurs when a malicious force, often a malevolent human spirit or a demonic entity, overtakes a person or location, often resulting in dysfunction, suffering, and persecution.

orb: in supernatural terms an anomaly often seen in photographs or videos and, rarely, with the naked eye. Orbs are often round and may be either translucent or one of many colors. Some people believe that orbs are the manifestations of ghosts or spirits, but in truth, the vast majority of orb anomalies are caused by environmental contaminants, such as dust, flying insects, moisture in the air, or camera malfunctions.

Ouija board (trademark: Hasbro, Inc.): commonly used name for a divination tool that consists of a flat board generally marked with the letters of the alphabet, the numbers 0–9, and the words "yes," "no," "hello," and "good-bye." Other symbols and words are sometimes added to help personalize the board. Users of the board place their fingers lightly on a wooden planchette (a small, heart-shaped wooden object) or other similar device that moves about the board—theoretically as the result of manipulation by a ghost or spirit—to spell out a message. Originally designed as a harmless parlor game, Ouija boards are now widely feared due to the belief that their use opens up the possibility for negative energies to manifest. This fear of Ouija boards was undoubtedly, in part, perpetuated by its unfavorable appearances in films such as *The Exorcist* and *Witchboard*.

out-of-body experience (OBE or OOBE): the unintentional act of the spirit (or soul or consciousness) leaving the physical body. (*See also* astral projection, near-death experience)

Ovilus: an electronic device (also a smart phone app) created by engineer Bill Chappell and used by many paranormal investigators. The Ovilus contains a database of words and an EMF (electromagnetic field) detector that work in tandem to generate what some consider to be messages from disincarnate beings.

paranormal: describes events or phenomena that defy rational or scientific principles and understanding. Paranormal = can't understand it, can't explain it, can't deny it. (Frequent synonyms: "supernatural," "preternatural," "occult")

parapsychology: the study of psychological phenomena, such as telepathy, clairvoyance, and psychokinesis, that are scientifically inexplicable.

pareidolia: *See* matrixing

poltergeist: (German for "noisy ghost") a very active disincarnate being who is frequently malicious or malevolent.

possession: held by many religions and belief systems to be the control of an individual by a malevolent supernatural being, often a demon. Demonic possession is not recognized as a medical or psychological disorder, but a number of psychological ailments, such as dissociative identity disorder, are commonly misunderstood as demonic possession. In cases of dissociative identity disorder in which the alternate personality is questioned as to its identity, 29 percent are reported to identify themselves as demons, but doctors see this as a mental disease called demonomania or demonopathy, in which the patient believes that he or she is possessed by one or more demons. (*See also* exorcism)

precognition: unexplainable knowledge of something in advance of its occurrence.

premonition: a presentiment of the future; a foreboding or forewarning.

psychic: (noun) an individual who is able to access information and energy that cannot be accessed by using the five human senses; (adjective) of or pertaining to supernatural abilities. (Frequent synonyms: "intuitive," "sensitive")

psychokinesis: the paranormal ability to affect matter with the mind. Examples of psychokinesis include distorting or moving an object and influencing the outcome of a random-number generator. (Frequent synonym: "telekinesis")

Reiki: (Japanese for "spirit life force") a form of energy healing founded in Japan. Practitioners of Reiki seek to manipulate the *ki*, or life force, in themselves and/or others, thus facilitating healing. (Frequent synonyms for *ki*: in China, "chi"; in India, "*prana*")

reincarnation: the rebirth of a soul in a new body.

residual haunting: unexplainable supernatural activity that seemingly occurs as the result of strong emotions or powerful acts that have occurred in certain locations, e.g., the appearance of ghostly soldiers on battlefields. Residual hauntings are thought to be energetic imprints or echoes. This type of haunting does not involve any form of conscious interaction between living beings and the ghostly beings involved in the haunting. (*See also* intelligent haunting)

runes: Germanic and/or Nordic alphabet symbols used in a form of divination that usually employs stones inscribed with various runic symbols, whose meaning is said to reveal the future or aid in decision-making.

schizophrenia: a mental disorder characterized by the disintegration of thought processes and emotional responsiveness that most frequently manifests in young adulthood. It most commonly manifests as auditory hallucinations, paranoid or bizarre delusions, or disorganized speech and thinking. Schizophrenia is accompanied by significant social or occupational dysfunction. Psychic children have frequently been misdiagnosed as schizophrenic.

scrying: the act of seeing things physically in certain reflective, translucent, or luminescent media, such as crystals, stones, water (and other liquids), glass, mirrors, fire, and smoke, usually for purposes of obtaining spiritual visions and less often for purposes of divination or fortune-telling. Depending on the culture and practice, the visions that come when one stares into the medium are thought to come from God, spirits, the psychic mind, the devil, or the subconscious. The most popular items used for scrying are mirrors and crystal balls.

sensitive: someone with a heightened sense of awareness and the ability to receive paranormal or supernatural information and messages. (Frequent synonyms: "psychic," "intuitive")

sixth sense: psychic ability and/or intuition; individuals who have knowledge of or information about that which is not accessible using the five standard human senses are often referred to as having a sixth sense.

sleep paralysis: a physiological condition that occurs when an individual is falling asleep or waking up, lasting from several seconds to several minutes, characterized by a sense of being unable to move or of being held down. Other symptoms may include vivid hallucinations and an acute sense of danger. Typically, but not always, sleep paralysis occurs when a person is sleeping on his back. Those who experience sleep paralysis often say they have the feeling that someone or something—often described as a demon or old hag—is sitting on their upper body. This hallucinatory state has given rise to folklore that exists throughout the world. Possible causes for sleep paralysis include increased stress, sudden environmental or lifestyle changes, lucid dreaming that immediately precedes the episode, and excessive consumption of alcohol coupled with sleep deprivation. Many who experience sleep paralysis also suffer from narcolepsy, the excessive urge to fall asleep at inappropriate times.

soul: the life force or essence of being that resides within all living creatures.

spirit: *See* ghost

spirit guide: a disincarnate being who guides, assists, and sometimes protects the living. From my own perspective, spirit guides are beings who have lived numerous lifetimes on the earthly plane, learned valuable soul-enriching karmic lessons, and are tasked with co-creating a meaningful lifetime existence for the living. Most people have numerous spirit guides, some of whom will remain with their soul throughout numerous human incarnations. Although an individual's spirit guides may be part of his soul's "spirit family," it is not common for living people to have known their spirit guides during their current incarnation.

star children: *See* indigo children

supernatural: of or relating to existence outside the natural world; of or relating to a deity; of or relating to that which is seemingly impossible, unbelievable, or miraculous; that which is attributed to a source or power that seems to violate or go beyond natural forces. (Frequent synonyms: "paranormal," "occult")

tarot cards: a specialized deck of cards, traced back to fifteenth-century Europe, that is commonly used for purposes of divination and fortune-telling. Most tarot decks contain seventy-eight cards, divided into four suits of fourteen cards (the standard ace through ten, then page, knight, queen, and king) and twenty-two unnumbered triumphs or trumps. The four suits are commonly called the Minor Arcana and the trump cards are called the Major Arcana.

telekinesis: *See* psychokinesis

telepathy: the transference of thought; nonverbal communication of thoughts, images, etc.

teleportation: paranormal transference of an object to a distant location.

walk-ins (or spirit walk-ins): believed by some to be disincarnate energies who have work they need to do in the material world but do not want or need to incarnate into the flesh for an entire lifetime. Instead, the walk-in occupies the body of an already-living being. When the soul that "owns" a body has finished its work on the earthly plane and is ready to die or "return to spirit," in some instances a walk-in is allowed to "sublet" the body. Once the walk-in has taken up residence in the host's body, changes in personality are frequently noticed by others.

white noise: any repetitive or droning sound or noise, such as the sound of rain falling, ocean waves, or the hum of an electric fan. In paranormal research, white noise is a term often ascribed to a hisslike sound formed by combining various audible frequencies.

Some believe that disincarnate beings may use the sounds or vibrations generated by white noise to facilitate auditory communication.

wraith: a ghost or ghost-like image, especially one that is seen shortly before or after a person's death.

(The following Internet sites were used to assist with some definitions: en.Wikipedia.org and thefreedictionary.com.)

PRAYERS OF PROTECTION

The majority of the following prayers are from the Christian tradition. They are the prayers I use, but if there are others in your own faith that work for you, by all means use them. There is no prayer that works better than any other; God protects us all however we reach out to Him.

THE LORD'S PRAYER

Our Father who art in heaven, hallowed be Thy name. Thy kingdom come, Thy will be done on earth as it is in heaven. Give us this day our daily bread and forgive us our trespasses as we forgive those who trespass against us. And lead us not into temptation, but deliver us from evil. For Thine is the kingdom and the power and the glory, forever. Amen.

PRAYER TO SAINT MICHAEL THE ARCHANGEL

Saint Michael the archangel, defend us in battle. Be our protection against the wickedness and snares of the devil. May God rebuke him, we humbly pray. And do thou, O prince of the heavenly host, by the power of God, thrust into hell Satan and all evil spirits who wander throughout the world seeking the ruin of souls. Amen.

PSALM 23

The Lord is my shepherd, I shall not want. He maketh me to lie down in green pastures. He leadeth me beside the still waters. He restoreth my soul. He leadeth me in the paths of righteousness for His name's sake. Yea, though I walk through the valley of the shadow of death, I will fear no evil, for Thou art with me. Thy rod and Thy staff, they comfort me. Thou preparest a table before me in the presence of mine enemies. Thou anointest my head with oil. My cup runneth over. Surely, goodness and mercy shall follow me all the days of my life. And I will dwell in the house of the Lord forever. Amen.

THE PRAYER OF JABEZ (I CHRONICLES 4:10)

And Jabez called on the God of Israel, saying: "Oh, that You would bless me, indeed, and enlarge my territory. That Your hand would be with me, and that You would keep me from evil, that I may not cause pain." So, God granted him what he requested. Amen.

PSALM 71:1–3

In You, O, Lord, I take refuge. Incline Your ear to me and save me. Be my rock of refuge, a stronghold to give me safety. Amen.

IF YOU ARE EXPERIENCING A TROUBLESOME OR MALICIOUS HAUNTING, THE FOLLOWING PRAYER IS A VERY POWERFUL TOOL TO USE AGAINST NEGATIVE ENTITIES

Exorcizo te, immundissime spiritus . . . in nomine Domini nostri Jesu Christi.

(Translation: "I exorcize you, unclean spirit . . . in the name of our Lord Jesus Christ.")

Phonetically: *Ex-or-see-so tay, em-moon-diss-uh-mee speer-e-toos, in nom-en-ay Doh-men-ee no-stree Yay-sue Kris-tee.*

—From the Roman Catholic rites of exorcism, found in the *Rituale Romanum*

ROMANS 12:21

Do not be overcome by evil, but overcome evil with good.

TRUE TALES I NEVER TIRE
OF TELLING

WITH A LITTLE HELP FROM MY FRIENDS

Did Demons Force Mark David Chapman to Murder John Lennon?

I remember I was praying to God [to keep me from killing Lennon] and I was also praying to the devil to give me the opportunity. 'Cause I knew I would not have the strength on my own. —Mark David Chapman

On December 8, 1980, at 10:50 P.M., John Lennon was brutally gunned down in New York City as he was returning home from a recording session. Twenty-five-year-old Mark David Chapman fired five hollow-point rounds from a .38 revolver at Lennon. Four of the bullets hit their target. The fatal shot pierced the former Beatle's aorta. Lennon was declared dead at 11:15 P.M. after losing more than 80 percent of his blood.

As the news of Lennon's death quickly spread, millions of people were stunned and grief stricken. Memorial vigils were held in cities around the world. Even though the legend and the music of John Lennon would live on, his life had come to a tragic end.

Much has been written about Mark David Chapman's troubled life prior to that fateful day in December of 1980, but few people know about the supernatural events that occurred several years earlier in DeKalb County, Georgia, that may have played a major role in the murder of John Lennon.

HELTER SKELTER

Maria Simpson* first met Mark David Chapman in 1972 when he was working as a volunteer youth counselor at the YMCA in Decatur, a suburb of Atlanta. According to Maria, everyone adored Mark. The children he worked with nicknamed him "Nemo," referring to the character in the Jules Verne novel *Twenty Thousand Leagues Under the Sea*.

Maria's daughter, Cathy, was a quiet, shy seven-year-old child who had difficulties with eye-hand coordination. "Mark took her under his wing and taught her how to swim and to shoot a bow and arrow," Maria remembers.

Maria; her husband, Harold; and their two children resided in a four-bedroom, two-story house in Decatur. The Simpsons moved there in 1971 and within two weeks, strange things started to happen.

---

*At the "Simpson" family's request, their names have been changed to protect their privacy.

Maria vividly remembers the first occurrence. "One afternoon, I was lying on the couch in the living room, taking a nap. I was exhausted from all the unpacking and needed to take a break. Suddenly, I felt something hit me and I awoke to discover that Cathy had dropped the bathroom scale on me. She was standing over me, smiling, as if [she was] very pleased by what she had done. My nose was bleeding and I asked her, 'Why on earth did you do that to me?' She did not respond. Later in the day, Cathy snapped out of her trancelike state with absolutely no recollection of what she had done."

Soon after that incident Cathy began waking up every night at eleven o'clock, screaming and crying. She would stand on her bed, yelling and sweating profusely, her eyes wide open, with a wild look on her face. One night, when Maria came in to comfort her, Cathy screamed, "There's an old man standing behind you!" When Maria turned to look, she found no one there. At least no one *she* could see.

Cathy's behavior grew even more bizarre. She began cursing, which she had never done before, and even began to violently attack others. Fearful for her daughter's physical and mental health, Maria took Cathy to a pediatrician, who found nothing wrong with the child's general state of health. The pediatrician referred them to a neurologist, who suspected that Cathy might be suffering from psychomotor epilepsy and prescribed phenobarbital and Dilantin.

The nightly episodes subsided a bit but did not stop entirely. One night, Cathy told her mother that she saw the old man standing outside her bedroom window, which was physically impossible, given the fact that her bedroom was on the second story of the house. Another night, Maria awoke when she heard an unusual noise and found Cathy sitting on top of her sleeping younger brother, Matthew, holding a pillow over his face.

Some time after that a friend of Matthew's came to visit, and when he left he vowed never to go back. From that day forward he always referred to the Simpsons' home as "the black house," which was odd because the exterior of the house was painted white. Years later, as a teenager, the boy suddenly began having nightmares about the Simpsons' house and sought help from a therapist.

Also, while playing outside one day, Maria's children and their friends found some bones in the crawl space under the house. "They brought them in to show them to me," Maria remembers. "Of course, I told the children they were the bones of an animal, but I wasn't sure."

In 1976, the Simpson family relocated to upstate New York for a year because of Harold Simpson's job, but they did not sell the house in Decatur. During the year they were away from Georgia, Cathy exhibited no bizarre behavior at all.

When they returned to Decatur, however, all hell broke loose! Toilets began flushing, faucets would turn on, and lights would switch on and off, all without the aid of a human hand. Maria recalls hearing strange whisperings and music inside the house and smelling cologne, an old-fashioned scent worn by no one living in the house.

One night, while her husband was out of town on a business trip, Maria returned home after having dinner with a female friend. As they got out of the car, both women saw a man standing in the window of the bathroom. Terrified that someone was burglarizing the house, they telephoned the friend's husband, who rushed over, searched the house, and found no one.

Maria had never believed in the supernatural or paranormal, but now she was starting to suspect that something "unseen and unknown" had invaded her home. Her husband, a logical and pragmatic man, tried to reassure her that there had to be rational explanations for everything that had happened, but she was not convinced.

Whatever had taken up residence in the Simpsons' home angrily refused to be discounted or discredited. Late one evening, Maria heard a loud noise outside that sounded like someone repeatedly hitting the house with a sledgehammer. Books began flying off the shelves and a candlestick slid across the buffet.

Desperate for answers and assistance, she called a Catholic priest, who came out to bless the house. "There is definitely an evil presence here," the priest told her. She then sought help from a paranormal investigator and a psychic, who agreed that there was "something very negative" in the Simpsons' home.

Maria Simpson and her family finally moved from the house in Decatur to a new home in Gwinnett County in 1979. Thankfully, whatever had been haunting their former residence did not follow them to their new home. Cathy Simpson never again suffered from bizarre or violent behavior.

MADMAN

Mark David Chapman was born in Fort Worth, Texas, on May 10, 1955. When he was a small child, the Chapman family moved first to Indiana, then to Georgia. Mark told psychiatrists who examined him years later that his childhood had been "unhappy." He said that his father had never shown him any love or emotional support and also claimed that his father had been physically abusive to his mother.

Mark was an intelligent boy, with an above-average IQ of 121. Adults considered him a "normal" child, but other children frequently picked on him and called him ugly names.

Slowly, Mark began to retreat into a world of fantasy where he was completely in control. In a biography of Mark written by Jack Jones, Mark says, "I used to fantasize that I was a king, and I had all these Little People around me and that they lived in the walls. And that I was their hero and was in the paper every day and I was on TV every day, their TV, and that I was important. They all kind of worshipped me, you know. It was like I could do no wrong."

Mark often held concerts for his loyal and faithful subjects. His favorite recordings—and theirs—were songs by the Beatles.

But Mark was not always a benevolent ruler. "Sometimes, when I'd get mad, I'd blow some of them up. I'd have this push-button thing, part of the [sofa], and I'd, like, get mad and blow out part of the wall and a lot of them would die. But the people would still forgive me for that, and, you know, everything got back to normal. That's a fantasy I had for many years," he told his biographer.

At the age of fourteen, Mark began experimenting with illegal drugs and exhibiting antisocial behavior. Then, two years later, this period of rebellion ended abruptly when he attended an evangelical church service and became a born-again Christian.

While in high school, Mark began volunteering at the local YMCA. He was well liked by his supervisors, coworkers, and especially the children he worked with, including Cathy and Matthew Simpson. Mark dated and eventually became engaged to a young woman named Jessica Blankenship. His life seemed to be progressing nicely and he was happy. Unfortunately, that happiness would be short-lived.

Around this same time, a friend suggested that he read *The Catcher in the Rye*, which recounts the story of Holden Caulfield, a troubled youth who is rather aimlessly trying to find his way in a world filled with insurmountable obstacles and countless "phonies." Mark immediately saw the similarities between his own life and the life of Holden Caulfield. He became completely obsessed with the book.

Mark enrolled as a student at Covenant College, a strict Presbyterian school in Lookout Mountain, Tennessee, but when he began falling behind in his studies, he finally gave up and dropped out. His relationship with Jessica also began to disintegrate and she broke off their engagement. Depression, along with chronic thoughts of suicide, took hold of him. In his opinion, he was a complete failure. A nobody.

In the years between 1977 and 1980, Mark David Chapman moved from Georgia to Hawaii, where he attempted suicide and was hospitalized. Following his stay in the hospital he was hired to work there as a maintenance man. When Mark discovered that he could borrow money from the hospital's credit union, he took out a loan and requested a six-week leave of absence. He began planning a trip to the Far East with the assistance of a travel agent named Gloria Abe, with whom he developed a personal relationship.

After traveling around the world, Mark returned to Atlanta, where he visited with family and friends, including the Simpsons.

Maria Simpson remembers Mark's visit very well. "We drove up to the house and found Mark sitting in the backyard. I was so happy to see him. I hugged him and told him, 'Oh, it's so good to see you, Nemo!' Mark pulled away from me and said, 'Don't call me that! Don't ever call me Nemo again!' I was surprised by his reaction and said, 'Okay . . . why don't you want to be called Nemo anymore?' Mark replied, 'Because Nemo means nothing. It means zero.'

"My daughter, Cathy, had always idolized Mark, but this time, she wanted nothing to do with him," Maria says. "She hid behind me the entire time Mark was there. I thought maybe she was just being a typical adolescent girl and acting shy. So I asked her, 'Don't you want to give Mark a hug?' She shook her head and whispered to me, 'He's different. I'm afraid of him!'" Maria did not disagree with her daughter's assessment of Mark.

When he finally returned to Hawaii, Gloria was there waiting for him. He asked her to marry him and they were wed in June of 1979. It has been speculated that Mark's decision to marry Gloria may have been made due to a twisted sense of reverence for John Lennon, because both Gloria and John's wife, Yoko Ono, are of Japanese descent.

Sadly, Mark's life once again began to unravel. He was fired from his job at the hospital, was subsequently rehired, then quit after having a shouting match with a nurse. Following a heated argument with Gloria's boss at the travel agency, he also made his wife quit her job.

Mark's descent into darkness escalated. He both idolized and loathed John Lennon, often listening to Beatles music, yet furious that Lennon preached love and peace while earning millions of dollars. He decided that Lennon must die and that he should be the one to kill him.

I'LL GET YOU

In 1987, James R. Gaines wrote an eighteen-thousand-word article about Mark David Chapman that was published in *People* magazine. During the interview for the article, Mark told Gaines that he had begun to pray to Satan. "There were no candles, no incantations," Gaines wrote. "Just Mark, sitting naked, rocking back and forth at the controls of his stereo and tape recorder, splicing together his reasons for killing John Lennon from the lyrics of Beatles songs, the sound track of *The Wizard of Oz*, and quotations from *The Catcher in the Rye*."

Mark told his Little People he intended to go to New York and kill John Lennon. They begged him fervently not to do so. "Please, think of your wife. Please, Mr. President. Think of your mother. Think of yourself." He told them that his mind was made up. Their reaction was silence.

Mark knew that John Lennon, his wife, and their son, Sean, lived in the Dakota, an upscale apartment building located on the Upper West Side of New York. Methodically, he began to formulate his plan.

THE LONG AND WINDING ROAD

On October 27, 1980, Mark went to a gun shop in Honolulu and bought a five-shot, short-barrel .38-caliber handgun for $169. Ironically, the man who sold him the gun was named Ono.

On October 30, wearing a new suit and topcoat, with the revolver in his suitcase, he boarded a plane for New York.

When he arrived, Mark spent most of the day walking around the Dakota, studying its entrances and exits. He asked the doorman if John and Yoko were in town and received the standard reply, "I don't know."

Mark had forgotten to buy bullets for his gun before leaving Hawaii and was distressed to learn that New York State law prohibited him from buying them there. He called Dana Reeves, an old friend in Atlanta who worked as a sheriff's deputy, and told Reeves that he was coming for a visit. Dana invited Mark to stay at his apartment, and Mark boarded a plane for Atlanta.

While in Atlanta, he told Dana that he had purchased a handgun for his own protection and needed some bullets "with real stopping power." Dana provided Mark with five hollow-point cartridges, the kind that expand as they pass through their target.

Maria Simpson remembers that sometime in the late fall of 1980 she received a telephone call from a former neighbor who told her that she had seen Mark Chapman "sitting in a swing in the yard of [their] old house." Maria says, "I had no idea why he had gone there. He knew we had moved."

Is it possible that the demons dwelling in that house had summoned Mark, taunting him and commanding him to carry out a deadly deed in New York City?

Once he had secured the bullets he needed and had paid a visit to the Simpsons' former home, Mark returned to New York, arriving on November 10. The following night, he had an epiphany while watching the movie *Ordinary People* at a local theater. In the film, a teenage character named Conrad Jarrett, portrayed by Timothy Hutton, is plagued with problems and attempts suicide. Mark felt that watching the movie somehow changed him. He left the theater and called Gloria in Hawaii. In the course of their conversation, he whispered to her that he planned to kill John Lennon. Gloria begged Mark to come home. And he did.

Mark returned to Hawaii, but his reprieve was short-lived. The demons returned in full force, and Mark soon began making threatening phone calls, making bomb threats, and harassing a group of Hare Krishnas who gathered regularly in downtown Honolulu. After spending less than a month in Hawaii, Mark told Gloria that he was returning to New York. She begged him not to, but on December 6, 1980, he was back in the Big Apple.

HAPPINESS IS A WARM GUN

He spent the better part of the next two days outside the Dakota, watching and waiting. On the afternoon of December 8 he was awestruck when, at around four P.M., he saw John and Yoko leaving the building.

As they walked toward their limousine, which was at the curb, Mark shook hands with John, then handed him a copy of John's new album, *Double Fantasy*, for him to sign. Lennon graciously autographed the album cover for Mark, then, ironically, asked him twice, "Is that all you want?" Did John Lennon somehow sense that there was something more to this encounter than simply a fan seeking an autograph?

Reportedly, the paranormal and the occult fascinated John and Yoko. They frequently consulted with psychics, but it is not known if any of their psychic advisers made predictions regarding John's tragic fate.

After John and Yoko left, Mark continued to wait near the Dakota. The part of Mark David Chapman that remained good and sane begged him to take his autographed album and leave, but the demons commanded him to stay and carry out his task. The demons were victorious.

Around 10:50 P.M., John and Yoko returned. They got out of their limousine and walked toward their apartment building. The demons inside Mark's head began screaming, over and over again, "Do it! Do it! Do it!"

Just as John and Yoko approached the entrance archway, Mark dropped into a military firing stance and called out, "Mr. Lennon?" When John turned to see who had called his name, Mark fired his gun five times. Lennon turned to escape, but four of the five bullets ripped into him. To Mark's amazement, he did not collapse but managed to run up six steps into the concierge's station and yell, "I'm shot!" before falling facedown. Less than twenty-five minutes later, John Lennon was pronounced dead.

Members of the New York City Police Department apprehended Mark without incident. He was charged with second-degree murder and taken to Bellevue Hospital for psychiatric examination. The windows in his room were painted black because authorities feared snipers would try to assassinate him.

Within days, he was transferred to Rikers Island, New York City's largest prison facility. While at Rikers, Mark underwent examination by a number of psychiatrists, who concluded that although he was clearly delusional, he was competent to stand trial.

The diagnoses provided by the psychiatrists, however, differed. Some stated that Mark was decidedly psychotic, while others said that his delusions were not severe enough to categorize him as suffering from psychosis.

Originally, as advised by his defense attorney, Mark entered a plea of not guilty by reason of insanity. Then, on June 8, 1981, just two weeks before his trial was scheduled to begin, he informed his lawyer that he wanted to change his plea to guilty. There are conflicting reports as to why Mark made this decision. One version states that Mark said, "God wants me to do so." Another version says that Mark claimed, "The little voices inside my head told me to plead guilty."

Maria Simpson was stunned when she heard that Mark had murdered John Lennon. "My reaction was one of shock and disbelief. I thought, 'There must be some mistake. Nemo wouldn't do such a thing!'"

Soon after the killing, Maria received a call from the police in New York City. Mark had told them to contact her, saying, "She knows me better than anyone else." The police informed Maria that Mark stated he had committed the murder because two demons he encountered in the Simpsons' home ordered him to do it. He called the demons by the names of Lila and Dobar.

"I begged the police not to share that part of the story with the media," Maria said. "I was afraid some angry or grieving fan might try to harm me or my family because of our association with Mark."

On August 24, in a packed New York City courtroom, Judge

Dennis Edwards sentenced Mark David Chapman to a term of twenty years to life for the murder of John Lennon. He would not be eligible for parole until the turn of the millennium.

HEAR ME, LORD

During his interview for the 1987 *People* magazine article, Mark talked about an incident that had occurred shortly after he was imprisoned at Attica Correctional Facility near Buffalo, New York. He said he felt the Holy Spirit come down and say that there were demons inside him. "And I asked in Jesus' name [for them to come out]," Mark said. "My face was snarling and it came out my mouth, this *thing*, and it was gone. And I said, 'I'm ready, God, let's get 'em all out, let's go.' During that hour, six came out. [They were] the most fierce and incredible things you ever saw or heard in your life. Hissing, gurgling noises and different voices right out of my mouth. The way I was acting, cursing and things like this, weren't me, and when they came out, I could sense these things coming out of my mouth, hissing and awful gurgling and grinding and I could feel that part of my personality was gone."

Maria Simpson was mentioned in the *People* magazine article and she also appeared in a BBC documentary about the infamous case. Since then, she has rarely spoken of her connection to Mark David Chapman. "It all happened so long ago," Maria said with a troubled sigh. "We [she and her family and friends] don't talk about it much anymore." Maria does admit, however, that, through the years, she has thought about calling Mark, but finally decided that "it's best to just let it be."

Almost three decades after he killed John Lennon, Mark David Chapman remains imprisoned at Attica, completely separated from other inmates because of concerns for his safety. He is a model prisoner who reads and watches television in his tiny six-by-ten-foot cell. Mark has been denied parole three times and it is almost certain that he will remain in prison until his own death.

He claims that he is now free from the demons who ordered him to kill his onetime hero.

The family who purchased the house in Decatur from the Simpsons in 1979 still live there. They refuse to discuss any unusual experiences they may have had in the house. Maria did have an opportunity, many years ago, to speak with one of the twin daughters of the couple who purchased the house. "I asked [the child] if anything strange had ever happened in the house. She told me that, once, she saw an old man standing on the stairs." Maria shuddered when she realized that the demons might still be living in the house!

DO YOU WANT TO KNOW A SECRET?

Undeniably, the most frightening and compelling facet of this story is something that Maria Simpson has thought about many times since Mark David Chapman killed John Lennon. "Even though Mark was very close to me and my family, no one ever spoke to him about the strange incidents that took place at the house in Decatur. There was absolutely no way he could've known about the 'demons' that invaded our home . . . unless he had encountered them himself."

Bibliography and Acknowledgments

Wikipedia articles on Mark David Chapman and John Lennon

"The Man Who Shot Lennon" by James R. Gaines, *People*, February/March 1987

Let Me Take You Down: Inside the Mind of Mark David Chapman, the Man Who Killed John Lennon by Jack Jones, Villard, 1992

Mark David Chapman: The Man Who Killed John Lennon by Fred McGunagle, from Court TV's Crime Library website http://www.trutv.com/library/crime/terrorists_spies/assassins/chapman/1.html

HONORING ADAM

In the spring of 2002, I received a call from a woman named Anna who asked me to contact her deceased husband, Adam.

Immediately, images of September 11, 2001, began to flash in my mind. "Did Adam die on 9/11?" I asked Anna.

"Yes, he did," she told me.

During this very emotional reading, I discovered that Adam had perished when the north tower of the World Trade Center collapsed soon after American Airlines Flight 11 crashed into the building. Adam had been attending a business meeting at Windows on the World, the restaurant located atop the tower, that morning.

Adam provided Anna with a great deal of information that was meaningful to her, but undoubtedly the most profound message was that he was okay, that his soul had crossed over into the spirit world and he was at peace.

At the end of our conversation, Anna and I agreed to stay in touch. I mentioned to her that I felt the need to someday visit Ground Zero, and she told me that if and when I did visit, she would like to go with me.

She said there was an office space in a nearby building that had been set aside exclusively for family members and friends of those who died at the World Trade Center. "From the windows of the office, you can look right down on the site," she told me. "I can take you there if you want to go."

Several weeks later, I phoned Anna to tell her that I would be visiting New York City for some business meetings and asked if she was still interested in going to Ground Zero with me.

We met in the lobby of my hotel and we gave each other a big hug. After a short taxi ride, we arrived at the office building where the memorial suite was located. After passing through heavy security, which included Anna's having to provide a special number that was given to her as proof that she'd lost a loved one when the towers fell, we rode the elevator to an upper floor and entered the suite.

The walls were completely covered with photographs, religious objects, and other items that had been placed there by the loved ones of those who died on 9/11. I was overcome with emotion, barely able to breathe.

"You can see the site from those windows over there," Anna said softly, nodding toward a huge bank of windows at the far end of the room. Instinctively, at precisely the same moment, we reached out and took each other's hands, walking together toward the windows.

As I looked down on the site where the two majestic towers once soared into the sky, tears streamed down my face. I felt the sadness and the loss, but then a new emotion swept over me: peace.

In my mind, I saw thousands of angels flocking to the World Trade Center on that awful September morning. God had sent them there to take away the souls of those who died . . . far, far away from the horror and devastation.

"Adam isn't here anymore. He's gone from this place," I told his grieving wife. She smiled back at me through her own tears.

Before leaving the memorial suite, I took a few moments to kneel in prayer, asking God to continue to heal the souls of those who had died there and the souls of those who were left behind, their lives devastated by the loss of those they love.

Riding back down on the elevator, I asked Anna what she and Adam would do on this bright, sunny morning if they were together in the here and now. She laughed and said, "We'd probably go over to Blimpie's for his favorite, a Blimpie Best combo, and have lunch together in the little park across the street."

And that is precisely what we did, in honor of Adam.

After lunch Anna and I walked together for a few blocks; then I hailed a cab for her, hugged her tightly, and said good-bye. As the taxi disappeared into traffic, I somehow knew that Anna would find ways to go on with her life without her beloved husband.

RIDING IN THE BIG RED TRUCK

The moment that the three women entered the room, I sensed that each of them was carrying a great burden of sadness and grief. One of the women, Connie, had phoned me earlier in the week to schedule an appointment for herself, her sister, and their mother. They had driven more than two and a half hours from their home in rural Alabama to have their sitting with me.

"I would like you to try to communicate with my daughter, Jessica. She died a month ago," Connie told me, her voice filled with emotion.

Whenever a client informs me that she wishes to communicate with a recently departed spirit—someone who has passed away within several weeks of the time of the sitting—I become a bit concerned. Sometimes, because of a lengthy and debilitating illness, or if the death is sudden and unexpected, the soul is weakened and/or fragmented once it leaves the body and needs a period of recuperation and recovery. I have been told by my spirit guides that there are loving beings in the spirit world who work with these "damaged" souls in order to make them well and "whole" again. During that "settling in" period, it can be difficult to establish a clear connection with their spirit energy.

That was not the case with the recently departed Jessica, however. Her spirit energy came rushing up to me immediately, and without a doubt I knew that she had been very young when she died.

In my mind, I saw a beautiful little girl, small and frail, with no hair on her head. I described what I was seeing to the women who were sitting with me and two of them began to cry. Only Connie's mother—Jessica's grandmother—remained stoic and dry-eyed.

I saw tubes and wires and machines . . . medical equipment. I sensed that Jessica had died because of a blood disorder. "Did Jessica die of leukemia?" I asked. Connie nodded yes.

I delivered several more messages that seemed to be meaningful to Jessica's mother and her aunt, but still her grandmother remained rigid and expressionless, sitting with her arms crossed. "Grandma doesn't believe," Jessica told me.

"You don't believe in what we're doing here, do you?" I asked Jessica's grandmother.

"No, I really don't," she admitted. "My daughters begged me to come here with them and I agreed because I wanted to be supportive."

For the next few minutes, every message that Jessica sent through to me was a message for her grandmother. She showed me very special moments that they'd shared when Jessica was alive. As I described what I was seeing, tears began to flow down the grandmother's cheeks.

She unfolded her arms, slumped over, buried her face in her hands, and wept as the bitterness, anger, and grief she felt over the loss of her precious granddaughter gave way to other powerful emotions.

Shortly before our sitting ended, Jessica asked me to tell her family she was "riding in the big red truck." I had no idea what the message meant, but it was obvious that the women knew.

"When Jessie was so sick, we used to play her a song about riding over the rainbow in a big red fire truck. She always smiled when she heard that song," Connie told me.

As we said good-bye, I hugged each of the women, and Jessica's grandmother whispered to me, "I'm sorry I doubted you."

"No need to apologize," I told her with a smile. "Please, just know in your heart that Jessie is okay."

Later that night, I received a voice mail from Connie. "I'm just calling to thank you again. Our reading with you was an absolute miracle," she said to me. And then she told me something that made me cry.

On the way back home to Alabama, as the women were talking about the reading, a huge rainbow suddenly arched across the sky. "It was as if God and Jessie were letting us know that she really is all right," Connie said, sobbing.

REUNIONS

Back in the 1970s, I attended and graduated from Elmira College in upstate New York. Elmira is a small, private school, so it was quite easy to get to know many of the other students on campus.

One of my classmates was a girl named Norma. She and I worked together on many shows that were produced by the theater department, so we became good friends.

Shortly after graduation, I lost touch with Norma, but I often read updates about her in the college's alumni magazine and heard stories via the "Elmira grapevine." Norma married and she and her husband, Michael, had one son, Matthew. Matthew was the light of their lives, a great kid who was an Eagle Scout and well-loved in their community north of New York City.

Tragically, Matthew was killed when he was just eighteen years old in an automobile accident. The loss of their son devastated Norma and Michael.

Years later, as our thirty-fifth college reunion approached, I invited Norma to meet me in Elmira and told her that if she wanted me to, I would try to communicate with Matthew. She and Michael made the trip and we shared a lovely weekend, along with other classmates, at our reunion.

One night, a group of us got together to do a bit of ghost hunting in Tompkins Hall, a dormitory on campus with a history of haunted activity. At least a dozen of us were crammed into a small dorm room on the fourth floor, trying to make contact with the spirits of any former students who might be there.

One of the ways I attempt spirit communication is through the use of flashlights. I ask any spirits who wish to make their presence known to turn on the light. I learned this communication technique during a visit to Iron Island Museum, a haunted location in Buffalo, New York.

Try as we might, none of the dearly departed Elmira coeds seemed willing to light up either the red or purple flashlight that I regularly use when attempting this method of spirit contact. And then a thought came to me. "Perhaps we might be able to communicate with some of your deceased loved ones," I said to the group. "Are you all willing to try that?" Everyone seemed not only willing but also eager to do so.

Norma was sitting across the room from me and I asked her if it would be all right to reach out first to Matthew. She gave me permission, so I called out to Matthew, told him his mom was present in the room and that I'd spent time that weekend with her and his dad, who was downstairs relaxing in the dorm's great room. I told Matt that Norma and Michael loved him very much and they missed him. I asked him to turn on one of the flashlights if he could hear me.

Almost immediately, the red flashlight came on. Not only did it illuminate, the bulb began to pulse in a strobelike fashion! My first thought—and everyone present later agreed—was that Matt seemed very excited to be communicating with us.

I was totally amazed by the actions of the red flashlight. I have used it many times, in many locations, and never before had the light strobed like it did that night.

We asked Matt several questions, instructing him to light up the flashlight for "yes" answers and leave it off if the answer was "no." The responses were amazing and each time the answer was yes, the light flashed rapidly on and off.

Others in the room were anxious to attempt contact with their loved ones, so I asked Matt to help me bring them forward and teach them how to use the purple flashlight. "The red light is for your use only tonight, Matt," I told him.

During the following hour, with Matt's help, we communicated with several deceased loved ones of the individuals assembled in the room. Each time that Matt brought a spirit forward, he would strobe the red flashlight and moments later, the purple one would light up.

Many tears of joy were shed that night and we were all astounded by how precisely the flashlights had "performed."

Several months later, at one of my live Coffey Talk events, I shared with the audience the story of what had happened that special night at my reunion. As I was preparing to use my flashlights to demonstrate how it is possible to communicate with the spirit world, I decided to once again reach out to Matt, hoping he might be willing to help me bring forward some spirits.

Moments after I called out Matt's name, the red flashlight began to flash! And for the remainder of the evening, he served as my "spiritual assistant," regaling the audience by strobing the flashlight in response to my questions. Even the members of my tour crew, who had witnessed my using the flashlights dozens of times, were amazed by the way that the red flashlight behaved.

Many times since, I have sought Matt's help when demonstrating for audiences how to communicate with the spirit realm using a simple tool such as a flashlight. He's become my "sidekick" at many events and I never forget to tell him how much he is loved and missed by his mom and dad.

Recently, I received an e-mail from Matt's mom, Norma, sharing with me a story of how Matthew reached out to her at a very significant time and place:

Hi Chip, hope everything is going well with your busy life. By now I expect the book is well on its way to publication.

When we were in Elmira you told us to expect some kind of sign from Matt. Well, it finally happened. BIG TIME. Matt and I always tried to go to the zoo together when we both had the day off from school. The last time we went was Columbus Day, two months before the accident. That day, I made him promise me that no matter how grown up he got he would never be too old to go to the zoo with his Mom. Yesterday [Columbus Day] was a perfect day; I was off from school, so I decided to take myself to the zoo.

As I was walking around, I could feel that he was with me, but I thought to myself, "I'm greedy, I wish I could have some sort of concrete sign." So I started looking. I went around to all the places we used to go, and soon came to the main gift shop, a mandatory stop on any parent/child trip. I came to a rack of keychains. Near the bottom of the rack there was one keychain hanging on a peg, all by itself. The only one that wasn't part of a stack. It was swinging back and forth on the peg. None of the others was moving. I thought, "Okay, this must be it." Then I realized they were personalized keychains. Of course they were. I couldn't see the name on it, but I knew.

Not only were there names on the keychains, they were solar powered so that the name flashed on and off. Seriously, Matt, you couldn't find a neon arrow?!? Of course the flashing name was Matthew, the <u>only one</u> on the display. If that wasn't enough, on the back were [images of] a snow leopard, a lion and a tiger. All the Big Cats he had planned on working with.

What a show off! Matt and I spent a lovely day together.
I thought you would appreciate this.
Norma

Norma's e-mail made me shed a few happy tears. What are the odds that she'd find just one swinging, flashing keychain with the name "Matthew" on a rack at the zoo on a day that held special significance for her and her son? And how synchronistic is it that Matt chose to flash his name at his mom, just the way he excitedly flashes my red flashlight?

Matt, I never knew you when you were alive, but you've become very special to me, years after your death. I love you, buddy!

AND THEN THE FLOWER GREW

Sometimes in life, it's hard to have faith and keep believing when fate pummels us with heartache, pain, confusion, and uncertainty. When my precious mother died in 1998 after a long and debilitating illness, I found myself wondering why God would dump so much pain and grief on me. I was bitter and angry and I didn't know if I believed in anything anymore.

My mother loved gardenias, those delicate white blossoms that permeate the early summer air with their sweet fragrance. I remember buying her Jungle Gardenia cologne when I was a small child, just because it had the word "gardenia" on the bottle. The scent was rather pungent and a bit overpowering, but she loved it. Or at least she pretended to, because it was a gift from me.

Once, many years ago, during a surprisingly lighthearted conversation about death and dying, Mother informed me, "I want to be buried in a black dress, holding a rosary and a single white gardenia in my hands."

I smiled and told her she'd better plan to kick the bucket during gardenia season, that short span of time when the flowers bloom, before the heat and humidity of late summer make it impossible for the fragile blossoms to survive. "I don't want to have to go on a horticultural treasure hunt when I'm ass-deep in grief!" I told her. And we both laughed heartily.

After my father died in 1986, Mother sold her home in South Carolina and moved to Georgia to live with me. We lived in rental houses for several years; then, in 1995, I bought a lovely home in the northeast Atlanta suburbs for Mother and me.

We moved in during the wintertime and much to our delight, when spring arrived, we discovered that there were two beautiful gardenia bushes in the side yard. Sadly, Mother lived only long enough to enjoy the flowers from those bushes for three growing seasons.

Mother's health was never very good, and it continued to decline slowly but steadily. Finally, when she wasn't able to leave the house, I'd pick blossoms from the gardenia bushes, put them in a vase, and set them by her bedside. The sight and smell of those flowers never failed to bring a smile to her face and elicit sighs of pure delight.

As so often happens in life, plans change. Mother never wore that black dress, with a rosary and gardenia clutched in her lifeless hands. Later in life, we both decided that we wanted to be cremated when our earthly days were over. And indeed, Mother was cremated after she passed away on August 12, 1998. I was devastated by her death. No matter how intellectually prepared I might have been, I was completely unprepared for the emotional shock of losing her. I felt like a part of my soul had been cruelly ripped away from me.

Mercifully, a sense of numbness overtakes us when someone we love dies, and we muddle through life on autopilot for days, weeks, sometimes even months. Even though I have always been a firm believer in the afterlife, I found myself wondering where my mother was. Was she in a safe, peaceful, happy place? A place free from sickness and pain? I prayed for a sign, something unmistakable, to show me that even though her body had died, her soul lived on.

Late one afternoon in mid-September, just as the sun was setting, my dog, Bo, began to prance around, letting me know that he needed to go out. No matter how I tried to persuade him to go into "his" huge fenced backyard, Bo flatly refused to do so. He kept looking at his leash, which was hanging on the newel post of the stairs in the foyer, as he always did when he wanted to take a walk.

Finally, I surrendered to his demands and took him for a walk in the front yard. After he'd sniffed around a bit and "watered" several bushes, I figured he was ready to go back inside, but he most assuredly was not. I tried to coax him into following me, but he adamantly refused. Again, I acquiesced, and, tugging at his leash, Bo led me into the side yard and straight to the gardenia bushes.

In the fading light of that September day, what I saw literally took my breath away. One perfect white blossom was growing in the center of the bushes! I immediately tried to explain it away, but logic told me that gardenias simply do not bloom during September in the state of Georgia. And why would there be just one blossom? One perfect blossom.

My prayers had been answered. I had been given a sign so personal and so profound that I knew it came from beyond. Someplace safe and peaceful and happy.

We expect miracles to happen on a grand scale, but oftentimes they occur so very simply. Like when a special song suddenly plays on the radio. Or when a rainbow magically appears in the sky. Or when someone we pass on the street smiles at us when we are feeling sad and lost and alone.

I never really expected a miracle.

And then the flower grew.

RECOMMENDED READING

Echo Bodine, *A Still, Small Voice: A Psychic's Guide to Awakening Intuition*, New World Library

Echo Bodine, *The Gift: Understand and Develop Your Psychic Abilities*, New World Library

John Holland, *Born Knowing: A Medium's Journey—Accepting and Embracing My Spiritual Gifts*, Hay House

Dr. Raymond Moody, *Life After Life*, Random House

Dr. Raymond Moody, *Reunions: Visionary Encounters with Departed Loved Ones*, Ivy Books

Dr. Michael Newton, *Destiny of Souls: New Case Studies of Life Between Lives*, Llewellyn Publications

RECOMMENDED READING

Dr. Michael Newton, *Journey of Souls: Case Studies of Life Between Lives*, Llewellyn Publications

Dr. Therese Rando, *How to Go on Living When Someone You Love Dies*, Bantam

Jane Struthers, *The Psychic Bible: The Definitive Guide to Developing Your Psychic Abilities*, Sterling Publishing Company

Dr. Brian Weiss, *Many Lives, Many Masters: The True Story of a Prominent Psychiatrist, His Young Patient and the Past-Life Therapy That Changed Both Their Lives*, Fireside

Dr. Brian Weiss, *Through Time into Healing*, Fireside

ACKNOWLEDGMENTS

You helped me to stand tall and proud again
Not afraid to face life anymore
Stronger and more whole now than before
Accepting what is good and right
Refusing to be led astray by what is false and wrong
Not healed . . . not yet . . . but healing
And with each new dawn
That brightly shines its warm and glowing sunshine
Through the windows of my life
I grow and learn
And know that I am better now
For loving and for caring
And for being who I am
And all that I will surely someday be . . .
—Chip Coffey

Bob and Carolyn Coffey, my mother and father, for giving me life—I miss you both very much.

Aunt Polly and Uncle Kenny Ray, for loving me and making my life so much better than it would have been without the two of you.

Kenny Ray—my cousin, my "brother," and my housemate—I'd be lost without you.

Ellen Barry May, for more than forty-six years of friendship, love, and support . . . and for teaching me that in life you don't often get a "do-over"—"I love you in a place where there's no space or time."

Celia Compton Ulmer, for being my precious friend since we were six years old.

Marisu Wehrenberg, for a beautiful friendship that has lasted more than three decades and for throwing me a lifeline when I so desperately needed one.

Michelle Griffin, for always listening and always knowing the right things to say.

Patti Starr, for taking me on my first "official" ghost hunt, for teaching me how to be a paranormal investigator, and for being my good friend.

Jane Norwood, Betty Kane, and Charlotte Scott—three amazing women who taught me to believe in things beyond the five human senses.

Greta Refert, my travel companion/assistant and manager of my Coffey Shoppe online store.

Rebecca Rakoski, my client services manager.

Apryl Edwards, my talent manager.

Randall Edwards, my talent agent.

Mike Anderson, my Coffey Talk tour producer, and the staff at Trixstar Productions in Edmonton, Alberta, Canada.

Mary "Mare" Aelich, for being my friend and helping me with social networking.

Eileen Cope, my literary agent.

Judy Kern, for helping me to make this book a reality.

Julia Pastore and the lovely folks at Random House, for making one of my dreams come true.

All the wonderful people whose stories are shared in this book, including many amazing psychic kids and their families.

Betsy Schechter, George Plamondon, and my awesome friends at Picture Shack Entertainment in New York City.

The folks at A&E and the Biography Channel, including Elaine Frontain-Bryant, Barry Rosenberg, Lauren Bienvenue, Rob Sharenow, and David McKillop.

Everyone who worked on the production crews of *Psychic Kids, Paranormal State*, and *Celebrity Ghost Hunt*—you are the best!

Kelly Allen Uminski, for more than a decade of friendship and for arranging my very first Coffey Talk event.

Dave Schrader, for making the call that got the ball rolling.

Ryan Buell and the Paranormal Research Society.

My spirit guides and guardian angels, for their love, wisdom, and protection.

And above all, **GOD** . . . for everything!

ABOUT THE AUTHOR

Chip Coffey is an internationally acclaimed psychic, medium, spiritual counselor, paranormal investigator, and lecturer. He is the great-grandson of Minnie Sue Morrow Foster, a Native American medicine woman and shaman whose own unique gifts were widely hailed in the early twentieth century. (He is also distantly related to General Robert E. Lee and Thomas Coffey, an actor who performed with Edwin and John Wilkes Booth.)

Chip was born in upstate New York, spent much of his childhood in South Carolina, and now resides in the suburbs of Atlanta, Georgia.

Television shows he has appeared on include *Psychic Kids: Children of the Paranormal*, *Paranormal State*, *Celebrity Ghost Hunt*, *Good Morning America*, and *Larry King Live*.

www.chipcoffey.com